Frederick T. Hodgson

The Carpenters' Steel Square, and its Uses

being a description of the square, and its uses in obtaining the lengths and

bevels of all kinds of rafters, hips, groins, braces, brackets, purlings,

collar-beams, and jack-rafters

Frederick T. Hodgson

The Carpenters' Steel Square, and its Uses
being a description of the square, and its uses in obtaining the lengths and bevels of all kinds of rafters, hips, groins, braces, brackets, purlings, collar-beams, and jack-rafters

ISBN/EAN: 9783337368647

Printed in Europe, USA, Canada, Australia, Japan

Cover: Foto ©Andreas Hilbeck / pixelio.de

More available books at **www.hansebooks.com**

THE CARPENTERS'

Steel Square,

AND

ITS USES.

BEING A DESCRIPTION OF THE SQUARE, AND ITS USES IN OBTAINING
THE LENGTHS AND BEVELS OF ALL KINDS OF

RAFTERS, HIPS, GROINS, BRACES, BRACKETS, PUR-LINS, COLLAR-BEAMS, AND JACK-RAFTERS;

ALSO, ITS APPLICATION IN OBTAINING THE BEVELS AND
CUTS FOR HOPPERS, SPRING MOULDINGS, OCTAGONS,
STAIRS, DIMINISHED STILES, ETC., ETC., ETC.

ILLUSTRATED BY OVER SEVENTY WOOD-CUTS.

BY

FRED. T. HODGSON,

Editor of the " Builder and Woodworker."

Second Edition.   Revised and Greatly Enlarged.

——— ▬ ———

NEW YORK:
THE INDUSTRIAL PUBLICATION COMPANY.
1883.

PREFACE TO SECOND EDITION.

THE rapid disposal of the first edition of the "STEEL SQUARE AND ITS USES," has rendered it incumbent for the publisher to issue a second and larger edition; and recognizing this condition, in connection with the fact that the work has met with more than a passing favor from those who make daily use of the Steel Square, it has been deemed necessary to make the present edition more useful by adding a number of solutions of mechanical problems by aid of the instrument, and other matters that will render the work more valuable to the operative mechanic.

The Author has reason to, and does, feel pleased at the appreciation the working mechanics of this country have evinced for this work; and is assured, by the numerous letters, and other indications of good feeling he has received on all hands, that the present enlargement of the work has not been made unnecessarily or too soon.

Feeling confident that the additions to the present edition will commend themselves to the toiling thousands who have daily use for the "Steel Square," the publishers send the enlarged work out to the public with a knowledge that it will be welcomed by those who are most interested in the subject of which it treats.

New York, Jan. 1, 1883.

PREFACE.

Some time ago, the author of this little work contributed a series of papers on the Steel Square and Its Uses, to the *American Builder*, and since their appearance, he has received hundreds of letters from as many persons residing in various parts of the United States, Canada, Australia and New Zealand, in which the writers requested him to publish the papers in book form. Partly in compliance with these requests, and partly at the solicitation of personal friends, together with a knowledge that a cheap but thorough work of the kind, would be of service to all persons who have occasion to use a steel square, he has consented, with the aid of the present enterprising publishers, to issue the work as now offered.

It is only of late years that American workmen have begun fully to understand the capabilities of the steel square; and even now, only a few of the best workmen have any idea of what can be accomplished with it when in skilful hands.

It is not claimed that the rules and methods shown in this little work are either new or original; they have been known to advanced workmen for many years past; but it is claimed that they have never before been brought together and put in so handy a shape as

v

In the present book; and it is further claimed that many of the rules herein illustrated and explained, have never appeared in print previous to the publication of the papers on the subject in the magazine referred to above.

Should this little volume prove of service to the man who toils with axe, saw and plane, for his daily bread, and profitable to the publishers who risk their money on its publication, it will have fulfilled its mission, as designed by

THE AUTHOR.

New York, 1880.

CONTENTS.

PART I.

PART II.

PART III.

PART IV.

THE CARPENTERS' STEEL SQUARE,

AND ITS USES.

PART I.

Preliminary.—There is nothing of more importance to a young man who is learning the business of house-joinery and carpentry, than that he should make himself thoroughly conversant with the capabilities of the tools he employs. It may be that, in some of the rules shown in this work, the result could be attained much readier with other aids than the square ; but the progressive mechanic will not rest satisfied with one method of performing operations when others are within his reach.

In the hand of the intelligent mechanic the square becomes a simple calculating machine of the most wonderful capacity, and by it he solves problems of the kinds continually arising in mechanical work, which by the ordinary methods are more difficult to perform.

The great improvement which the arts and manufactures have attained within the last fifty years, renders it essential that every person engaged therein should use his utmost exertions to obtain a perfect knowledge of the trade he

9

professes to follow. It is not enough, nowadays, for a person to have attained the character of a good workman; that phrase implies that quantum of excellence, which consists in working correctly and neatly, under the directions of others. The workman of to-day, to excel, must understand the principles of his trade, and be able to apply them correctly in practice. Such an one has a decided advantage over his fellow-workman; and if to his superior knowledge he possesses a steady manner, and industrious habits, his efforts cannot fail of being rewarded.

It is no sin not to know much, though it is a great one not to know all we can, and put it all to good use. Yet, how few mechanics there are who will know all they can? Men apply for employment daily who claim to be finished mechanics, and profess to be conversant with all the ins and outs of their craft, and who are noways backward in demanding the highest wages going, who, when tested, are found wanting in knowledge of the simplest formulas of their trade. They may, perhaps, be able to perform a good job of work after it is laid out for them by a more competent hand; they may have a partial knowledge of the uses and application of their tools; but, generally, their knowledge ends here. Yet some of these men have worked at this trade or that for a third of a century, and are to all appearances, satisfied with the little they learned when they were apprentices. True, mechanical knowledge was not always so easily obtained as at present, for nearly all works on the constructive arts were written by professional architects, engineers, and designers, and however unexceptionable in other respects, they were generally couched in such language, technical and mathematical, as to be perfectly unintelligible to the majority of workmen; and instead of acting as aids to the ordinary inquirer, they enveloped in mystery the simplest solutions of every-day problems, discouraging nine-tenths of workmen on the very threshold of inquiry, and causing them to abandon further efforts to master the intricacies of their respective trades.

Of late years, a number of books have been published, in which the authors and compilers have made commendable efforts to simplify matters pertaining to the arts of carpentry and joinery, and the mechanic of to-day has not the difficulties of his predecessors to contend with. The workman of old could excuse his ignorance of the higher branches of his trade, by saying that he had no means of acquiring a knowledge of them. Books were beyond his reach, and trade secrets were guarded so jealously, that only a limited few were allowed to know them, and unless he was made of better stuff than the most of his fellow-workmen, he was forced to plod on in the same groove all his days.

Not so with the mechanic of to-day; if he is not well up in all the minutæ of his trade, he has but himself to blame, for although there is no royal road to knowledge, there are hundreds of open ways to obtain it; and the young mechanic who does not avail himself of one or other of these ways to enrich his mind, must lack energy, or be altogether indifferent about his trade, and may be put down as one who will never make a workman.

I have thought that it would not be out of place to preface this work on the "Steel Square." with the foregoing remarks, in the hope that they may stimulate the young mechanic, and urge him forward to conquer what at best are only imaginary difficulties. A willing heart and a clear head will most assuredly win honorable distinction in any trade, if they are only properly used. Indeed, during an experience of many years in the employment and superintendence of mechanics of every grade, from the green "wood-haggler" to the finished and accomplished workman, I have invariably discovered that the finished workman was the result of persistent study and application, and not, as is popularly supposed, a natural or spontaneous production. It is true that some men possess greater natural mechanical abilities than others, and consequently a greater aptitude in grasping the principles that underlie the constructive arts; but, as a rule, such men are not reliable; they may be expert, equal to any mechanical emergency, and quick at mastering details, but they are seldom thorough, and never reliable where long sustained efforts are required.

The mechanic who reaches a fair degree of perfection by experience, study and application, is the man who rises to the surface, and whose steadiness and trustworthiness force themselves on the notice of employers and superintendents. I have said this in order to give encouragement to those young mechanics who find it up-hill work to master the intricacies of the various arts they are engaged in, for they may rest assured that in the end *work* and *application* will be sure to win; and I am certain that a thorough study of the steel square and its capabilities will do more than anything else to aid the young workman in mastering many of the mechanical difficulties that will confront him from time to time in his daily occupation.

It must not be supposed that the work here presented exhausts the subject. The enterprising mechanic will find opportunity for using the square in the solution of many problems that will crop up during his daily work, and the principles herein laid down will aid very much towards correct solutions. In framing roofs, bridges, trestle-work, and constructions of timber, the Steel Square is a necessity to the American carpenter; but only a few of the more intelligent workmen ever use it for other purposes than to make measurements, lay off the mortices and tenons, and square over the various joints. Now, in framing bevel work of any description, the square may be used with great advantage and profit. Posts, girts, braces, and struts of every imaginable kind may be laid out by this wonderful instrument, if the operator will only study the plans with a view of making use of his square for obtaining the various bevels, lengths and cuts required to complete the work in hand. Tapering structures—the most difficult the framer meets with—do not contain a single bevel or length that can not be found by the square when properly applied, and it is this fact I wish to impress on my readers, for it would be impossible, in this work, to give every possible application of the square to work of this kind. I have, therefore, only given such examples as will enable any one to apply some one of them to any work in hand.

The Square—Historical and Descriptive.—Doubtless, in the early ages of mankind, when solid structures became a necessity, the want of an instrument similar to the square must have been felt at every "turn and corner," and there can be no question about one having been used— rude and imperfect perhaps—in erecting the first square or rectangular building that was ever built on this earth.

The Greeks, who were an inventive people, and who were apt to ascribe to themselves more credit than was really their due, in the way of inventions and discoveries, lay claim to be the inventors of the instrument. Pliny says that Theodorus, a Greek of Samos, invented the square and level. Theodorus was an artist of some note, but it is evident that the square and level, in some form or other, were used long before his time, even in his own country, for some of the finest temples in Athens and other Grecian cities, had been built long before his time; and the Pyramids of Egypt were hoary with age when he was in swaddling cloths. Indeed, the "square," as a constructive tool, must of necessity have found a place in the "kit" of the earliest builders. Evidences of its presence have been found in the ruins of pre-historic nations, and are abundant in the remains of ancient Petra, Nineveh, Babylon, Etruria, and India. South American ruins of great antiquity in Brazil, Peru, and other places, show that the unknown races that once inhabited the South American Continent, were familiar with many of the uses of the square. Egypt, however, that cradle of all the arts, furnishes us with the most numerous, and, perhaps, the most ancient evidences of the use of the square; paintings and inscriptions on the rock-cut tombs, the temples, and other works, showing its use and application, are plentiful. In one instance, a whole "kit" of tools was found in a tomb at Thebes, which consisted of mallets, hammers, bronze nails, small tools, drills, hatchets, adzes, squares, chisels, etc.; one bronze saw and one adze have the name of Thothmes III., of the 18th dynasty, stamped on their blades, showing that they were made nearly 3,500 years ago. The constructive and decorative arts at that time were in their zenith in Egypt, and must have taken at least 1,000 years to reach that stage. Consequently, the square must have been used by workmen of that country, at least, four thousand years ago.

The British Museum contains many tools of pre-historic origin, and the square is not the least of them. Herculaneum and Pompeii contribute evidences of the importance of this useful tool. On some of the paintings recently discovered in those cities, the different artisans can be seen at home in their own workshops, with their work-benches, saw-horses, tools, and surroundings, much about the same as we would find a small carpenter shop of to-day, where all the work is done by hand; the only difference being a change in the form of some of the tools, which, in some instances, had been better left as these old workmen devised them.

It can make no difference, however, to the modern workman, as to when or where the square was first used; suffice to know, that, at present, we have squares immensely superior to anything known to the ancients, and it may be added, that so perfect has the machinery for the manufacture of steel squares become, that a defective tool is now the exception. Of course this relates to the products of manufacturers of repute, and not to the cheap squares, or to those said to be "first-class," that were made ten or fifteen years ago. The tool we recommend elsewhere is the best made, both as to quality of material, accuracy of workmanship, and amount of useful matter on its faces.

Description of the Square.—In the foregoing sketch I have given a few hints as to the kind of square to purchase when it is necessary to buy ; in many cases, however, this book will find its way into the hands of mechanics and others, who will have old and favorite squares in their chests or works! ops, and who will not care to dispose of a " well-tried .riend " for the purpose of filling its place with another, simply because I have recommended it. To these workmen I would say that I do not advise a change, provided the old square is true, and the inches and subdivisions are properly and accurately defined. I wish it distinctly understood that old squares, if true, and marked with inches and sub-divisions of inches, will perform nearly every solution presented in this book.

The lines and figures formed on the squares of different make, sometimes vary, both as to their position on the square, and their mode of application, but a thorough understanding of the application of the scales and lines shown on any first-class tool, will enable the student to comprehend the use of the lines and figures exhibited on other first-class squares.

To insure good results, it is necessary to be careful in the selection of the tool. The blade of the square should be 24 inches long, and two inches wide, and the tongue from 14 to 18 inches long and 1½ inches wide. The tongue should be exactly at right angles with the blade, or in other words the " square" should be perfectly square.

To test this question, get a board, about 12 or 14 inches wide, and four feet long, dress it on one side, and true up one edge as near straight as it is possible to make it. Lay the board on the bench, with the dressed side up, and the

trued edge towards you, then apply the square, with the
blade to the left, and mark across the prepared board with
a penknife blade, pressing close against the edge of the
tongue; this process done to your satisfaction, reverse the
square, and move it until the tongue is close up to the
knife mark; if you find that the edge of the tongue and
mark coincide, it is proof that the tool is correct enough
for your purposes.

This, of course, relates to the inside edge of the blade,
and the outside edge of the tongue. If these edges should
not be straight, or should not prove perfectly true, they
should be filed or ground until they 'are straight and true.
The outside edge of the blade should also be " trued" up
and made exactly parallel with the inside edge, if such
is required. The same process should be gone through
on the tongue. As a rule, squares made by firms of
repute are perfect, and require no adjusting; nevertheless,
it is well to make a critical examination before purchasing.

The next thing to be considered is the use of the figures,
lines, and scales, as exhibited on the square. It is supposed that the ordinary divisions and sub-divisions of the
inch, into halves, quarters, eighths, and sixteenths are understood by the student; and that he also understands
how to use that part of the square that is sub-divided into
twelfths of an inch. This being conceded, we now proceed
to describe the various rules as shown on all good squares;
but before proceeding further, it may not be out of place
to state, that on the tool recommended in this book, one
edge is subdivided into thirty-seconds of an inch.

This fine sub-division will be found very useful, particularly so when used as a scale to measure drawings made in

half, quarter, one-eighth, or one-sixteenth of an inch to the foot.

I now refer the reader to the square shown in the Frontispiece. It is the one recommended in the foregoing pages, and is the most complete square in the market, and manufactured, I believe, but by one firm. It is known to the trade as No. 100, and this number will be found stamped always on the face side of the square at the junction of the tongue and blade. The following instructions refer to the Frontispiece and accompanying cuts.

The diagonal scale is on the tongue at the junction with blade, Fig. 1, and is for taking off hundredths of an inch. The lengths of the lines between the diagonal and the

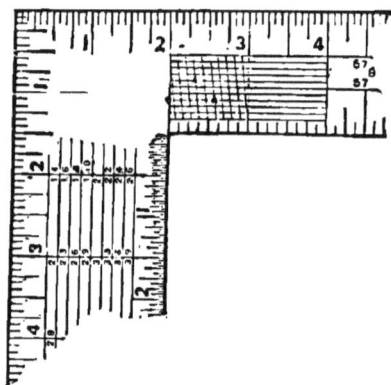

FIG. 2 a.

perpendicular are marked on the latter. Primary divisions are tenths, and the junction of the diagonal lines with the longitudinal parallel lines enables the operator to obtain divisions of one hundredth part of an inch; as, for example, if we wish to obtain twenty-four hundredths of an inch, we place the compasses on the "dots" on the fourth parallel line, which covers two primary divisions, and a fraction, or four-tenths, of the third primary division, which added together makes twenty-four hundredths of an inch. Again, if we wish to obtain five tenths and seven hundredths, we operate on the seventh line, taking five primaries and the fraction of the sixth where the diagonal intersects the parallel line, as shown by the "dots," on the compasses, and this gives us the distance required.

The use of this scale is obvious, and needs no further explanation.

Fig. 2 _a_ shows the position of the "dots" or "points" referred to in the foregoing example of the use of the diagonal scale.

Board, Plank and Scantling Measure.—Perhaps, with the single exception of the common inch divisions on the square, no set of figures on the instrument will be found more useful to the active workman than that known as the board rule. A thorough knowledge of its use may be obtained by ten minutes' study, and, when once obtained, is always at hand and ready for use.

The following explanations are deemed sufficiently clear to give the reader a full knowledge of the workings of the rule. If we examine Fig. 2, in the Frontispiece, we will find under the figure 12, on the outer edge of the blade, where the length of the boards, plank, or scantling to be measured, is given, and the answer in feet and inches is found under the inches in width that the board, etc., measures. For example, take a board nine feet long and five inches wide; then under the figure 12, on the second line will be found the figure 9, which is the length of the board; then run along this line to the figure

directly under the five inches (the width of the board), and
we find three feet nine inches, which is the correct answer
in "board measure." If the stuff is two inches thick, the
sum is doubled; if three inches thick, it is trebled, etc., etc.
If the stuff is longer than any figures shown on the square,
it can be measured by dividing and doubling the result.
This rule is calculated, as its name indicates, for board
measure, or for surfaces 1 inch in thickness. It may be
advantageously used, however, upon timber by multiplying
the result of the face measure of one side of a piece by its
depth in inches. To illustrate, suppose it be required to
measure a piece of timber 25 feet long, 10 x 14 inches in
size. For the length we will take 12 and 13 feet. For
the width we will take 10 inches, and multiply the result
by 14. By the rule a board 12 feet long and 10 inches

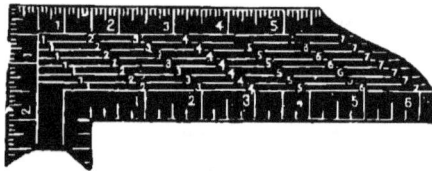

Fig. 3.

wide contains 10 feet, and one 13 feet long and 10 inches
wide, 10 feet 10 inches. Therefore, a board 25 feet long
and 10 inches wide must contain 20 feet and 10 inches.
In the timber above described, however, we have what is
equivalent to 14 such boards, and therefore we multiply
this result by 14, which gives 291 feet and 8 inches, the
board measure.

The "board measure," as shown on the portion of the

square, Fig. 3, gives the feet contained in each board according to its length and width. This style of figuring squares, for board measure, is going out of date, as it gives the answer only in feet.

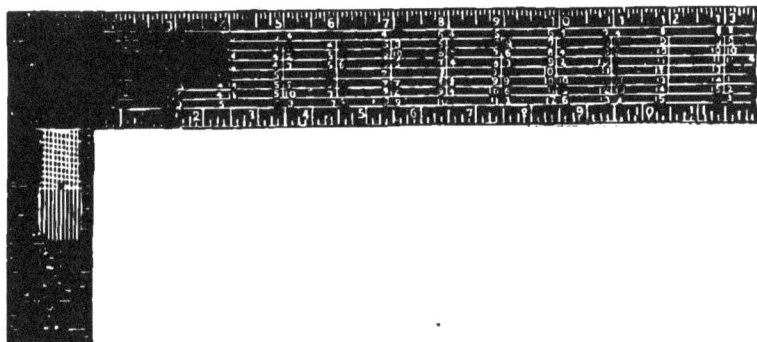

Fig. 3 *a*.

Fig. 3 *a* shows the method now in use for board measure. This shows the correct contents in feet and inches. It is a portion of the blade of the square, as shown at Fig. 2, on the Frontispiece.

Brace Rule.—The "brace rule" is always placed on the tongue of the square, as shown in the central space at x, Fig. 1.

This rule is easily understood; the figures on the left of the line represent the "run" or the length of two sides of a right angle, while the figures on the right represent the exact length of the third side of a right-angled triangle, in inches, tenths, and hundredths. Or. to explain it in another way, the equal numbers placed one above the other, may be considered as representing the sides of a square, and the third number to the right the length of the diagonal of that square. Thus the exact length of a brace from point to point having a run of 33 inches on a post, and a run of the same on a girt, is 46·67 inches. The brace rule varies somewhat in the matter of the runs expressed in different squares. Some squares give a few brace lengths of which the runs upon the post and beam are unequal.

Octagonal Scale.—The " octagonal scale," as shown on the central division of the upper portion of blade, is on the opposite side of the square to the " brace rule," and runs along the centre of the tongue as at s s. Its use is as follows : Suppose a stick of timber ten inches square. Make a centre line, which will be five inches from each edge ; set a pair of compasses, putting one leg on any of the main divisions shown on the square in this scale, and the other leg on the tenth subdivision. This division, pricked off from the centre line on the timber on each side, will give the points for the gauge-lines. Gauge from the corners both ways, and the lines for making the timber octagonal in its section are obtained. Always take the same number of spaces on your compasses as the timber is inches square from the centre line. Thus, if a stick is twelve inches square, take twelve spaces on the compasses; if only six inches square, take six spaces on the compasses, etc., etc. The rule always to be observed is as follows : Set off from each side of the centre line upon each face as many spaces by the octagon scale as the timber is inches square. For timbers larger in size than the number of divisions in the scale, the measurements by it may be doubled or trebled, as the case may be.

The diagram, Fig. 4 *a*, shows the application of the rule applied to the end of a stick of timber or on a plane surface. Let B C D E, be the square equal to six inches on a side. Draw the centre lines, B C and D E, then with the

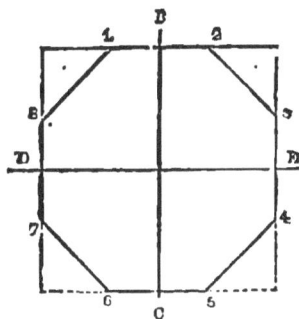

FIG. 4 *a*.

dividers take from the scale six parts, and lay off this distance from the centre of each; as B 1, B 2, E 3 and E 4, c 5 and c 6, D 7 and D 8. Draw lines from 1 to 8, 2 to 3, 4 to 5, 6 to 7, and the octagon figure is complete.

A rule for laying off octagons is figured on nearly all carpenters' two-foot rules, marked off from the inner edges of the rule; one set of figures is denoted by the letter E, another set is denoted by the letter M. That set marked E measures the distance from the edge of the square to the points indicated in the diagram, by the figures 1, 2, 3, 4, etc. The set marked M is used for finding the points 1, 2, 3, 4, etc., by measuring from the middle or centre lines, B, E, C, D.

I have now fully described all the lines, figures, and scales that are usually found on the better class of squares now in use; but, I may as well here remark that there are squares in use of an inferior grade, that are somewhat differently figured. These tools, however, are such as can not be recommended for the purposes of the scientific carpenter or joiner.

Fence.—A necessary appendage to the steel square in solving mechanical problems, is, what I call, for the want of a better name, an adjustable fence. This is made out of a piece of black walnut or cherry 2 inches wide, and 2 feet 10 inches long (being cut so that it will pack in a tool chest), and 1⅝ inches thick; run a gauge line down the centre of both edges; this done, run a saw kerf cutting down these gauge lines at least one foot from each end, leaving about ten inches of solid wood in the centre of fence. We now take our square and insert the blade in the saw kerf at one end of the fence, and the tongue in the kerf, at the other, the fence forming the third side of a right-angle triangle, the blade and the tongue of the square forming the other two sides. A fence may be made to do

FIG. 4.

pretty fair service, if the saw kerf is all cut from one end as shown at Fig. 4. The one first described, however, will be found the most serviceable. The next step will be to make some provision for holding the fence tight on the square ; this is best done by putting a No. 10 1½ inch screw in each end of the fence, close up to the blade and tongue ; having done this, we are ready to proceed to business.

Application.—The fence being made as desired, in either of the methods mentioned, and adjusted to the square, work can be commenced forthwith.

The first attempt will be to make a pattern for a brace, for a four-foot " run." Take a piece of stuff already prepared, six feet long, four inches wide and half-inch thick, gauge it three-eighths from jointed edge.

Take the square as arranged at Fig. 5, and place it on the prepared stuff as shown at Fig. 6. Adjust the square so that the twelve-inch lines coincide exactly with the gauge line o, o, o, c. Hold the square firmly in the position now obtained, and slide the fence up the tongue and blade until it fits snugly against the jointed edge of the prepared stuff, screw the fence tight on the square, and be sure that the 12 inch marks on both the blade and the tongue are in exact position over the gauge-line.

I repeat this caution, because the successful completion of the work depends on exactness at this stage.

We are now ready to lay out the pattern. Slide the square to the extreme left, as shown on the dotted lines at x, mark with a knife on the outside edges of the square, cutting the gauge-line. Slide the square to the right until the 12 inch mark on the tongue stands over the knife mark on the gauge-line ; mark the right-hand side of the square cutting the gauge-line as before, repeat the process four times, marking the extreme ends to cut off, and we have the length of the brace and the bevels.

Square over, with a try square, at each end from the gauge-line, and we have the toe of the brace. The lines, s, s, shown at the ends of the pattern, represent the tenons that are to be left on the braces. This pattern is now com-

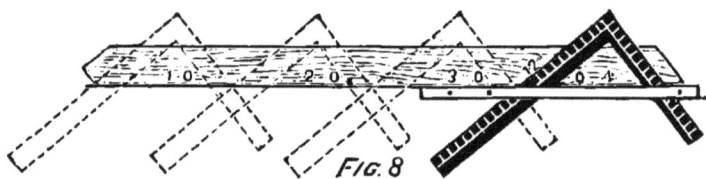

FIG. 8

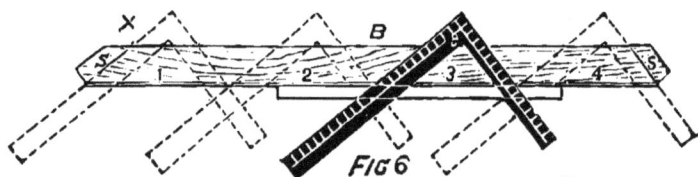

FIG 6

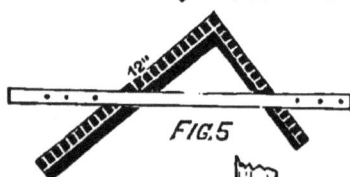

FIG. 5

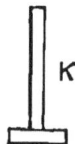

K

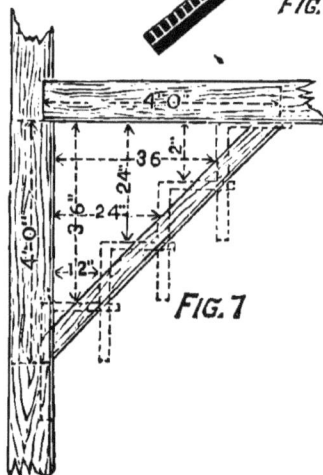

FIG. 7

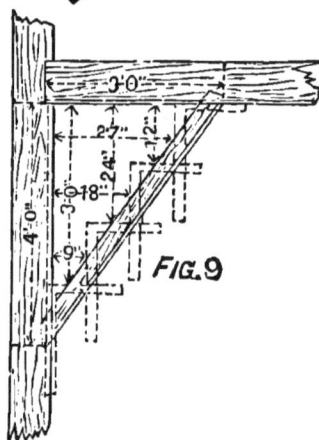

FIG. 9

plete ; to make it handy for use, however, nail a strip 2 inches
wide on its edge, to answer for a fence as shown at к, and
the pattern can then be used either side up.

The cut at Fig. 7, shows the brace in position, on a reduced scale. The principle on which the square works in
the formation of a brace can easily be understood from this
cut, as the dotted lines show the position the square was in
when the pattern was laid out.

It may be necessary to state that the " square," as now
arranged, will lay out a brace pattern for any length, if the
angle is right, and the *run* equal. Should the brace be of
great length, however, additional care must be taken in the
adjustment of the square, for should there be any departure
from truth, that departure will be repeated every time the
square is moved, and where it would not affect a short run, it
might seriously affect a long one.

To lay out a pattern for a brace where the run on the
beam is three feet, and the run down the post four, proceed
as follows :

Prepare a piece of stuff, same as the one operated on for
four feet *run;* joint and gauge it. Lay the square on the
left-hand side, keep the 12 inch mark on the tongue, over
the gauge-line, place the 9 inch mark on the blade, on the
gauge-line, so that the gauge-line forms the third side of a
right-angle triangle, the other sides of which are nine and
twelve inches respectively.

Now proceed as on the former occasion, and as shown
at Fig. 8, taking care to mark the bevels at the extreme
ends. The dotted lines show the positions of the square,
as the pattern is being laid out.

Fig. 9 shows the brace in position, the dotted lines show

where the square was placed on the pattern. It is well to thoroughly understand the method of obtaining the lengths and bevels of irregular braces. A little study, will soon enable any person to make all kinds of braces.

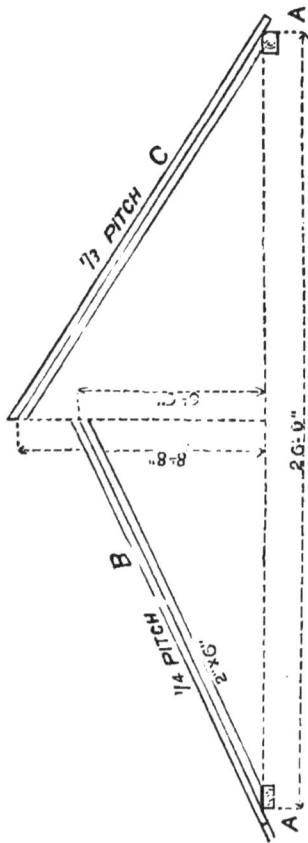

If we want a brace with a two feet run, and a four feet run, it must be evident that, as two is the half of four, so on the square take 12 inches on the tongue, and 6 inches on the blade, apply four times, and we have the length, and the bevels of a brace for this run.

For a three by four feet run, take 12 inches on the tongue, and 9 inches on the blade, and apply four times, because, as 3 feet is ¾ of four feet, so 9 inches is ¾ of 12 inches.

Rafters.—Fig. 10 shows a plan of a roof, having twenty-six feet of a span.

The span of a roof is the distance over the wall plates measuring from A to A, as shown in Fig. 10. It is also the extent of an arch between its abutments.

There are two rafters shown in position on Fig. 10. The one on the left is at an inclination of quarter pitch, and

marked B, and the one on the right,
marked C, has an inclination of one-third
pitch. These angles, or inclinations rather,
are called quarter and third pitch, respectively, because the height from level of wall
plates to ridge of roof is one-quarter or one-
third the width of building, as the case
may be.

At Fig. 11, the rafter B is shown drawn to
a larger scale; you will notice that this rafter
is for quarter pitch, and for convenience, it is
supposed to consist of a piece of stuff 2
inches by 6 inches by 17 feet. That portion
of the rafter that projects over the wall of the
building, and forms the eve, is three or more
inches in width, just as we please. The
length of the projecting piece in this case is
one foot—it may be more or less to suit the
eve, but the line must continue from end to
end of the rafter, as shown on the plan, and
we will call this line our working line.

We are now ready to lay out this
rafter, and will proceed as follows: We
adjust the fence on the square the same as
for braces, press the fence firmly against
the top edge of rafter, and place the figure
12 inches on the left-hand side, and the
figure 6 in on the right-hand side, directly
over the working line, as shown on the
plan. Be very exact about getting the
figures on the line, for the quality of the

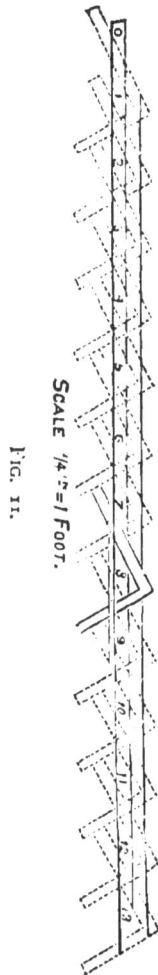

SCALE ¼″=1 FOOT.

FIG. 11.

work depends much on this; when you are satisfied that
you are right, screw your fence tight to the square. Com-
mence at No. 1 on the left, and mark off on the working
line; then slide your square to No. 2, repeat the marking
and cont'nue the process until you have measured off
thirteen spaces, the same as shown by the dotted lines in
the drawing. The last line on the right-hand side will be
the plumb cut of the rafter, and the exact length required.
It will be noticed that the square has been applied to the
timber thirteen times.

The reason for this is, that the building is twenty-six feet
wide, the half of which is thirteen feet, the distance that
one rafter is expected to reach, so, if the building was thirty
feet wide, we should be obliged to apply the square fifteen
times instead of thirteen. We may take it for granted,
then, that in all cases where this method is employed to
obtain the lengths and bevels, or cuts of rafters, we must
apply the square half as many times as there are feet in the
width of the building being covered. If the roof to be
covered is one-third pitch, all to be done is to take 12
inches on one side of the square and 8 inches on the other,
and operate as for quarter pitch.

We shall frequently meet with roofs much more acute
than the ones shown, but it will be easy to see how they
can be managed. For instance, where the rafters are at
right-angles to each other, apply the square the same as
for braces of equal run, that is to say, keep the 12 mark on
the blade, and the 12 mark on the tongue, on the working
line. When a roof is more acute, or "steeper" than a
right-angle, take a greater figure than twelve on one side
of the square, and twelve on the other,

Whenever a drawing of a roof is to be followed, we can soon find out how to employ the square, by laying it on the drawing, as shown in Fig. 12. Of course, something depends on the scale to which the drawing is made. If any of the ordinary fractions of an inch are used, the intelligent workman will have no difficulty in discovering what figures to make use of to get the "cuts" and length desired.

Sometimes there may be a fraction of a foot in this division; when such is the case, it can be dealt with as follows: suppose there is a fraction of a foot, say 8 inches, the half of which would be 4 inches, or ⅓ of a foot; then, if the roof is quarter pitch, all to be done is to place the square, with the 4 inch mark on the blade, and the 2 inch mark on the tongue, on the centre line of the rafter, and the distance between these points is the extra length required, and the line down the tongue is the bevel at the point of the rafter. On Fig. 13, is shown an application of this method. All other pitches and fractions can be treated in this manner without overtaxing the ingenuity of the workman.

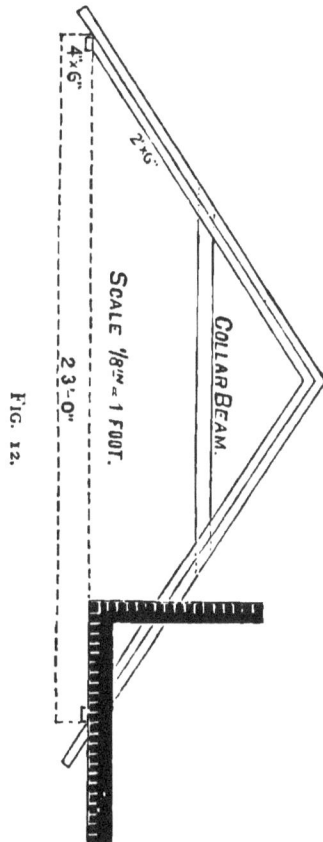

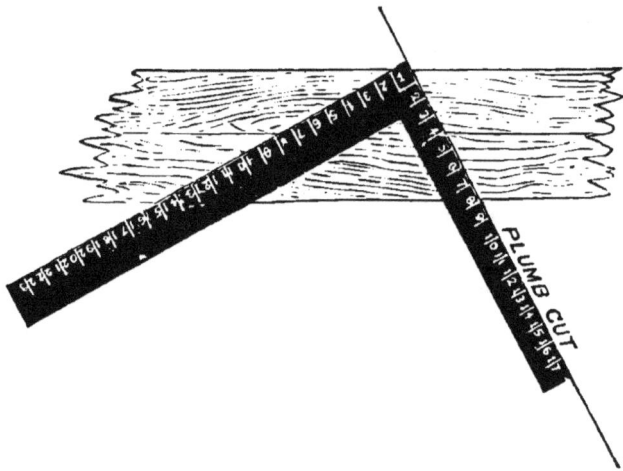

FIG. 14.

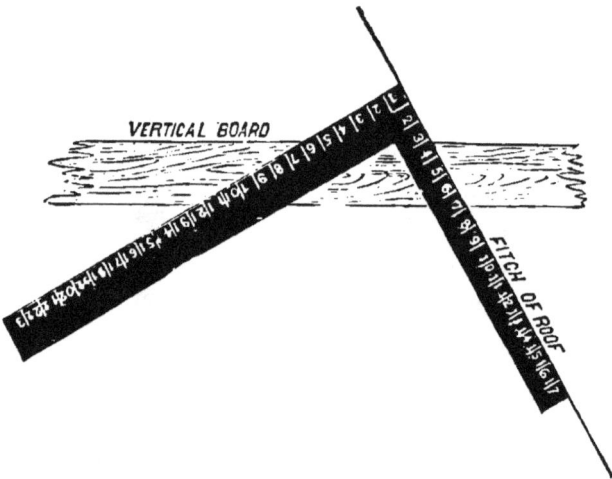

FIG. 14.

Sufficient has been shown to enable the student, if he has mastered it, to find the lengths and bevels of any common rafter; therefore, for the present, we will leave saddle roofs, and try what can be done with the square in determining the lengths and bevels of "hips," valleys, and cripples.

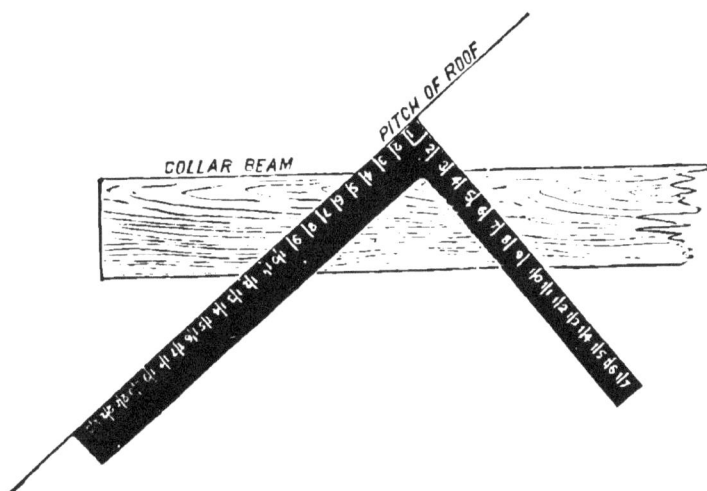

FIG. 15.

Fig. 14 shows how to get bevels on the top end of vertical boarding, at the gable ends, suitable for the quarter pitch at Fig. 10.

At Fig. 15, is shown a method for finding the bevel for horizontal boarding, collar ties, etc.

Hip Rafters.—Fig. 16, is supposed to be the pitch of a roof furnished by an architect, with the square applied to the pitch. The end of the long blade must only just enter

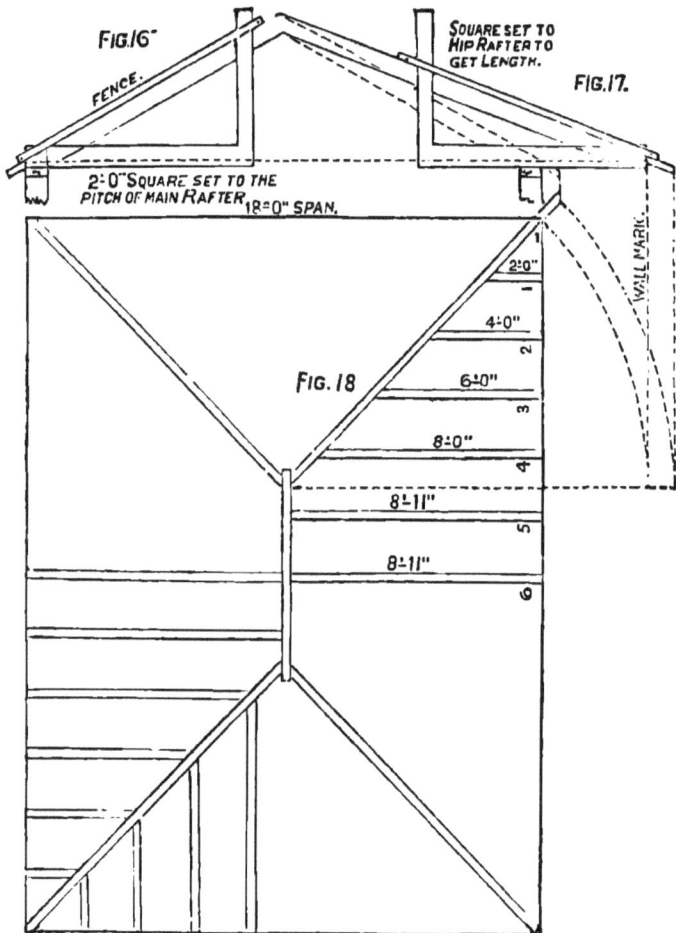

FIG.16

SQUARE SET TO
HIP RAFTER TO
GET LENGTH.

FENCE.

FIG.17.

2·0" SQUARE SET TO THE
PITCH OF MAIN RAFTER
18·0" SPAN.

WALL MARK.

FIG. 18

2·0"

4·0"

6·0"

8·0"

8·11"

8·11"

the fence, as shown in the drawing, and the short end must be adjusted to the pitch of the roof, whatever it may be. Fig. 17 shows the square set to the pitch of the hip rafter. The squares as set give the plumb and level cuts. Fig. 18 is the rafter plan of a house 18 by 24 feet; the rafters are laid off on the level, and measure nine feet from centre of ridge to outside of wall; there should be a rafter pattern with a plumb cut at one end, and the foot cut at the other, got out as previously shown. (Figs. 16, 17, 18, P.) When the rafter foot is marked, place the end of the long blade of the square to the wall line, as in drawing, and mark across the rafter at the outside of the short blade, and these marks on the rafter pitch will correspond with two feet on the level plan; slide the square up the rafter and place the end of the long blade to the mark last made, and mark outside the short blade as before, repeat the application until nine feet are measured off, and then the length of the rafter is correct; remember to mark off one-half the thickness of ridge-piece. The rafters are laid off on part of plan to show the appearance of the rafters in a roof of this kind, but for working purposes the rafters 1, 2, 3, 4, 5, and 6, with one hip rafter, is all that is required.

Hip-roof Framing.—We first lay off common rafter, which has been previously explained; but deeming it necessary to give a formula in figures to avoid making a plan, we take ⅓ pitch. This pitch is ⅓ the width of building, to point of rafter from wall plate or base. For an example, always use 8, which is ⅓ of 24, on tongues for altitude; 12, ½ the width of 24, on blade for base. This cuts common rafter. Next is the hip-rafter. It must be understood that the diagonal of 12 and 12 is 17 in framing, and the hip is the diagonal of a square added to the rise of roof; therefore we take 8 on tongue and 17 on blade; run the same number of times as common rafter (rule to find distance of hip diagonal $a^2 + a^2 + b^2 = y^2$). To cut jack rafters, divide the numbers of openings for common rafter. Suppose we have 5 jacks, with six openings, our common rafter 12 feet long, each jack would be 2 feet shorter. First 10 feet, second 8 feet, third 6 feet, and so on. The top down cut the same as cut of common rafter; foot also the same. To cut mitre to fit hip. Take half the width of building on tongue and length of common rafter on blade; blade gives cut. Now find the diagonal of 8 and 12, which is 14^{12}, call it 14 7-16, take 12 on tongue, 14 7-16 on blade; blade gives cut. The hip-rafter must be beveled to suit jacks; height of hip on tongue, length of hip on blade; tongue gives bevel. Then we take 8 on tongue 18¾ on blade; tongue gives the bevel. Those figures will span all cuts in putting on cornice and sheathing. To cut bed moulds for gable to fit under cornice, take half width of building on tongue length of common rafter on blade; blade gives cut; machine mouldings will not member, but this gives a solid joint; and to member properly it is necessary to make moulding by hand, the diagonal plumb cut differences. I find a great many mechanics puzzled to makes the cuts for a valley. To cut planceer, to run up valley, take heighth of rafter on tongue, length of rafter on blade; tongue gives cut. The plumb cut takes the height of hip-rafter on tongue, length of hip-rafter on blade; tongue gives cut. These figures give the cuts for ⅓ pitch only, regardless of width of building.

For a hopper the mitre is cut on the same principle.
To make a butt joint, take the width of side on blade, and
half the flare on tongue; the latter gives the cut. You
will observe that a hip-roof is the same as a hopper in-
verted. The cuts for the edges of the pieces of a hexagonal
hopper are found this way: Subtract the width of one
piece at the bottom from the width of same at top, take
remainder on tongue, depth of side on blade; tongue gives
the cut. The cut on the face of sides: Take 7-12 of the
rise on tongues and the depth of side on blade; tongue
gives cut. The bevel of top and bottom: Take rise on
blade, run on tongue; tongue gives cut.

Fig. 19 exhibits two methods of finding the "backing"
of the angle on hip-rafter. The methods are as simple as
any known. Take the length of the rafter on the blade,
and the rise on the short blade or tongue, place the
square on the line D E, the plan of the hip, the angle is
given to bevel the hip-rafter, as shown at F. This method
gives the angle, only for a right-angled plan, where the
pitches are the same, *and no other.*

The other method applies to right, obtuse, and acute
angles, where the pitches are the same. At the angle D
will be seen the line from the points K L, at the intersection of the sides of the angle rafter with the sides of the
plan.

With one point of the compass at D, describe the curve
from the line as shown. Tangential to the curve draw
the dotted line, cutting A, then draw a line parallel to A B,
the pitch of the hip. The pitch or bevel, will be found
at G, which is a section of the hip-rafter.

This problem is taken from "Gould's Carpenters'

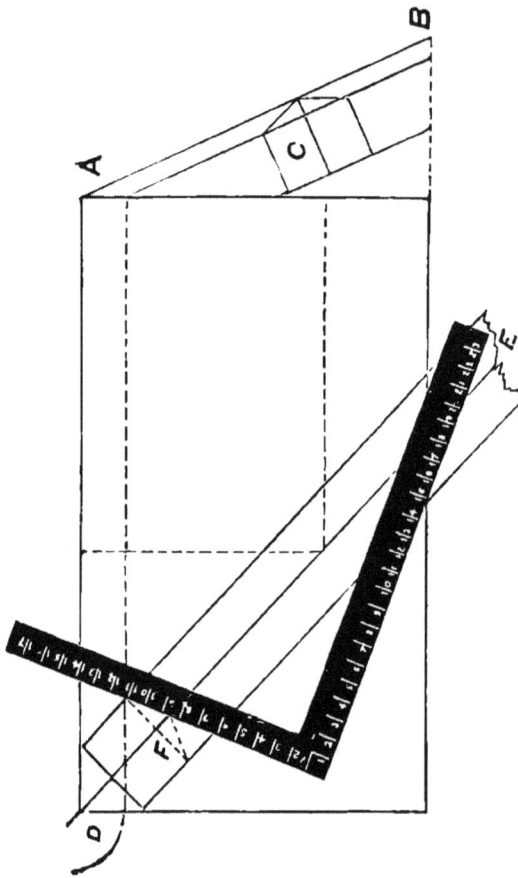

Fig. 12.

Guide," but has been in practice among workmen for many years.

FIG 20.

Fig. 20 exhibits a method of finding the cuts in a mitre box, by placing the square on the line A B at equal distances from the heel of the square, say ten inches. The bevel is shown to prove the truth of the lines by applying it to opposite sides of the square.

Stairs.—In laying out stairs with the square, it is necessary to first determine the height from the top of the floor on which the stairs start from, to the floor on which they are to land; also the "run" or the distance of their horizontal stretch. These lengths being obtained, the rest is easy.

Fig. 21 shows a part of a stair string. with the "square" laid on, showing its application in cutting out a pitch-board. As the square is placed it shows 10 inches for the tread and 7 inches for the rise.

To cut a pitch-board, after the tread and rise have been

determined, proceed as follows: Take a piece of thin, clear
stuff, and lay the square on the face edge, as shown in the
figure, and mark out the pitch-board with a sharp knife;

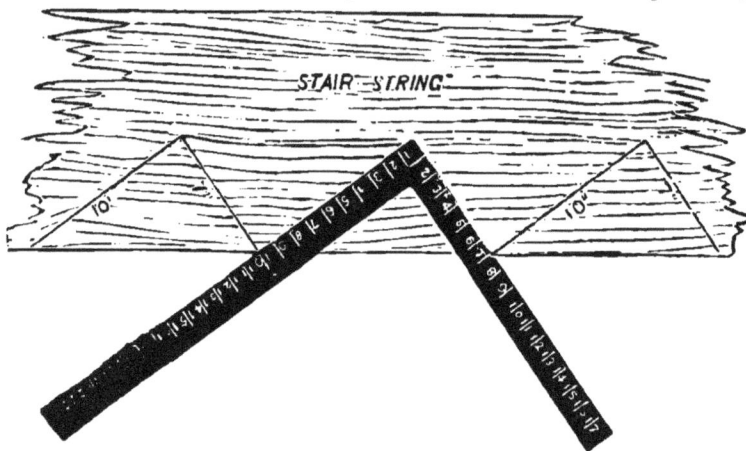

FIG. 21.

then cut out with a fine saw and dress to knife marks, nail
a piece on the longest edge of the pitch-board for a fence,
and it is ready for use.

Fig. 22 is a rod, with the number and heighth of steps
for a rough flight of stairs to lead down into a cellar or
elsewhere.

Fig. 23 is a step-ladder, sufficiently inclined to permit a
person to pass up and down on it with convenience. To
lay off the treads, level across the pitch of the ladder, set
the short side of the square on the floor, at the foot of the
string, after the string is cut, to fit the floor and trimmer
joists.   Fasten the fence on the square, as shown at Fig. 5.
The height of the steps in this case is nine inches, so it will
be seen that it is an easy matter to lay off the string, as the

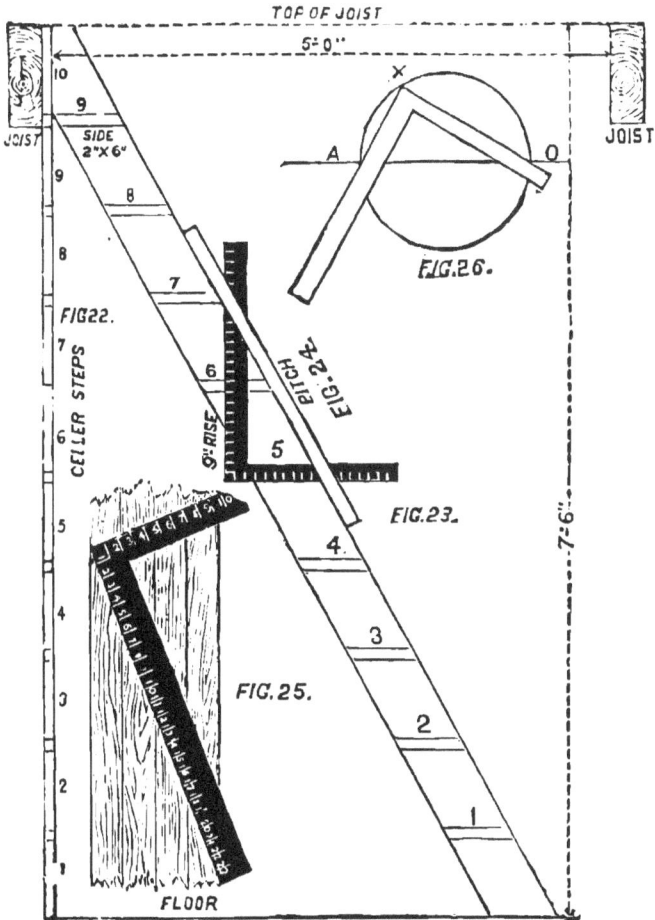

TOP OF JOIST

5ʼ-0ʻʻ

JOIST

JOIST

10

9

SIDE
2ʻʼX6ʻʼ

8

FIG22.

CEILER STEPS

7

6

5

4

3

2

1

9ʼʼRISE

PITCH

FIG.24.

FIG.23.

FIG.25.

FLOOR

X

A

O

FIG.26.

7ʼ-6ʻʻ

long side of the square hangs plumb, and nine inches up
its length will be the distance from one step to the next
one.

Fig. 24 shows the square and fence in position on the
string.

The opening in the floor at the top of the string shows
the ends of trimming joists, five feet apart.

Fig. 25 shows how to divide a board into an even number
of parts, each part being equal, when the same is an un-
even number of inches, or parts of an inch in width. Lay
the square as shown, with the ends of the square on the
edges of the board, then the points of division will be
found at 6, 12, and 18, for dividing the board in four
equal parts; or at 4, 8, 12, 16, and 20, if it is desired to
divide the board into six equal parts. Of course, the
common two-foot rule will answer this purpose as well
as the square, but it is not always convenient.

Fig. 26 shows how a circle can be described by means
of a " steel square " without having recourse to its centre.

At the extremities of the diameter, A, O, fix two pins, as
shown; then by sliding the sides of the square in contact
with the pins, and holding a pencil at the point x, a semicircle will be struck. Reverse the square, repeat the process, and the circle is complete.

Miscellaneous Rules —The following rules have been
tested over and over again by the writer, and found reliable
in every instance. They have been known to advanced
workmen for many years, but were never published, so far
as the writer knows, until they appeared in the *Builder and
Wood-Worker*, some years ago:

Measurement.—Let us suppose that we have a pile of lumber to measure, the boards being of different widths, and say 16 feet long. We take our square and a bevel with a long blade and proceed as follows: First we set the bevel at 12 inches on the tongue of the square, because we want to find the contents of the board in feet, 12 inches being one foot; now we set the other end of the bevel blade on the 16 inch mark on the blade of the square, because the boards are 16 feet long. Now, it must be quite evident to any one who would think for a moment, that a board 12 inches, or one foot wide, and 16 feet long, must contain 16 feet of lumber. Very well, then we have 16, the length, on the blade. Now, we have a board 11 inches wide, we just move our bevel from the 12 inch mark to the 11 inch mark, and look on the blade of the square for the true answer; and so on with any width, so long as the stuff is 16 feet long. If the stuff is 2 inches thick, double the answer, if 3 inches thick, treble the answer, etc.

Now, if we have stuff 14 feet long, we simply change the bevel blade from 16 inches on the square blade, to 14 inches, keeping the other end of the bevel on the 12 inch mark, 12 inches being the constant figure on that side of the square, and it will easily be seen that any length of stuff within the range of the square can be measured accurately by this method.

If we want to find out how many yards of plastering or painting there are in a wall, it can be done by this method quite easily. Let us suppose a wall to be 12 feet high and 18 feet long, and we want to find out how many yards of plastering or painting there are in it, we set the bevel on the 9 inch mark on the tongue (we take 9 inches because 9 square feet make one square yard,) we take 18 inches, one of the dimensions of the wall, on the blade of the square; then after screwing the bevel tight, we slide it from 9 inches to 12 inches, the latter number being the other dimension, and the answer will be found on the blade of the square. It must be understood that 9 inches must be a constant figure when you want the answer to be in yards, and in measuring for plastering it is as well to set the other end of the bevel on the figure that corresponds with the height of the ceiling, and then there will require no movement of the bevel further than to place it on the third dimension. This last rule is a very simple and very useful one; of course " openings " will have to be allowed for, as this rule gives the whole measurement.

If the diagonal of any parallelogram within the range of the square is required, it can be obtained as follows: Set the blade of the bevel on $8\frac{3}{4}$ in. on the tongue of the square, and at $12\frac{3}{8}$ in. on the blade; securely fasten the bevel at this angle. Now, suppose the parallelogram or square to be 11 inches on the side, then move the bevel to the 11 inch mark on the tongue of the square. and the answer, 15 9-16, will be found on the blade. All problems of this nature can be solved with the square and bevel as the latter is now set. There is no particular reason for using $8\frac{3}{4}$ and $12\frac{3}{8}$, only that they are in exact proportion to 70 and 99. $4\frac{3}{8}$ and 6 3-16 would do just as well, but would rot admit as ready an adjustment of the bevel.

To find the circumference of a circle with the square and bevel proceed as follows: Set the bevel to 7 on the tongue and 22 on the blade; move the bevel to the given diameter on the tongue of the square, and the approximate answer will be found on the blade. When the circumference is wanted the operation is simply reversed, that is, we put the bevel on the blade and look on the tongue of the square for the answer.

If we want to find the side of the greatest square that can be inscribed in a given circle, when the diameter is given, we set the bevel to $8\frac{1}{2}$ on the tongue and 12 on the blade. Then set the bevel of the diameter, on the blade, and the answer will be found on the tongue.

The circumference of an ellipse or oval is found by setting $5\frac{5}{8}$ inches on the tongue and $8\frac{3}{4}$ inches on the blade; then set the bevel to the sum of the longest and shortest diameters on the tongue, and the blade gives the answer.

To find a square of equal area to a given circle, we set the bevel to $9\frac{3}{4}$ inches on the tongue, and 11 inches on the blade; then move the bevel to the diameter of the circle on the blade, and the answer will be found on the tongue. If the circumference of the circle is given, and we want to find a square containing the same area, we set the bevel to $5\frac{1}{2}$ inches on the tongue and $19\frac{1}{2}$ inches on the blade.

On Fig. 27 is shown a method to determine the proportions of any circular presses or other cylinderical bodies, by the use of the square. Suppose the small circle, N, to be five inches in diameter and the circle R is ten inches in diameter, and it is required to make another circle, Z, to contain the same area as the two circles N and R. Measure line a, on the square D, from five on the tongue to 10 on the blade, and the length of this line A from the two points named will be the diameter of the larger circle Z. And again, if you want to run these circles into a fourth one, set the diameter of the third on the tongue of the square, and the diameter of z on the blade, and the diagonal will give the diameter of the fourth or largest circle, and the same rule may be carried out to infinite extent. The rule is reversed by taking the diameter of the greater circle and laying diagonally on the square, and letting the ends touch

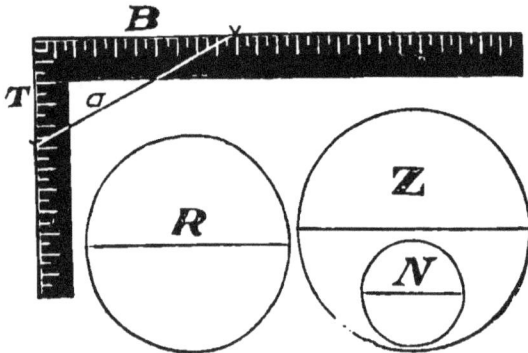

FIG. 27.

vhatever points on the outside edge of the square. These points will give the diameter of two circles, which combined, will contain the same area as the larger circle. The same rule can also be applied to squares, cubes, triangles, rectangles, and all other regular figures, by taking similar dimensions only; that is, if the largest side of one triangle is taken, the largest side of the other must also be taken, and the result will be the largest side of the required triangle, and so with the shortest side.

In Fig. 28 we show how the centre of a circle may be determined without the use of compasses; this is based on the principle that a circle can be drawn through any three points that are not actually in a straight line. Suppose we take A B C D for four given points, then draw a line from A

to D, and from B to C; get the centre of these lines, and
square from these centres as shown, and when the square
crosses, the line, or where the lines intersect, as at X, there
will be the centre of the circle. This is a very useful rule, and

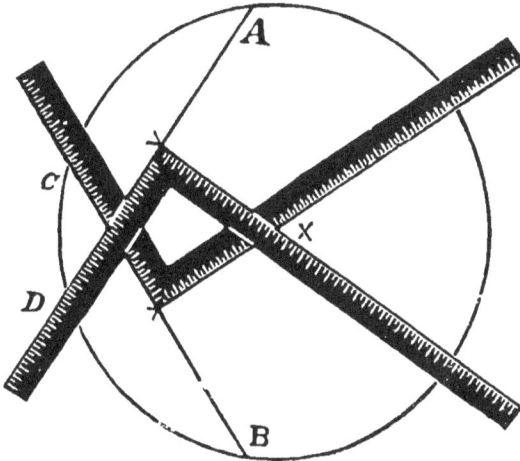

FIG. 28.

by keeping it in mind the mechanic may very frequently
save himself much trouble, as it often happens that it is necessary to find the centre of the circle, when the compasses
are not at hand.

In Fig. 29 we show how the square can be used, in lieu
of the trammel, for the production of ellipses. Here the
square, E D F, is used to form the elliptical quadrant,
A B, instead of the cross of the trammel; $h\ l\ k$ may be
simply pins, which can be pressed against the sides of the
square while the tracer is moved. In this case the adjustment is obtained by making the distance, $h\ l$, equal to the
semi-axis minor, and the distance $l\ k$, equal to the semi-axis
major.

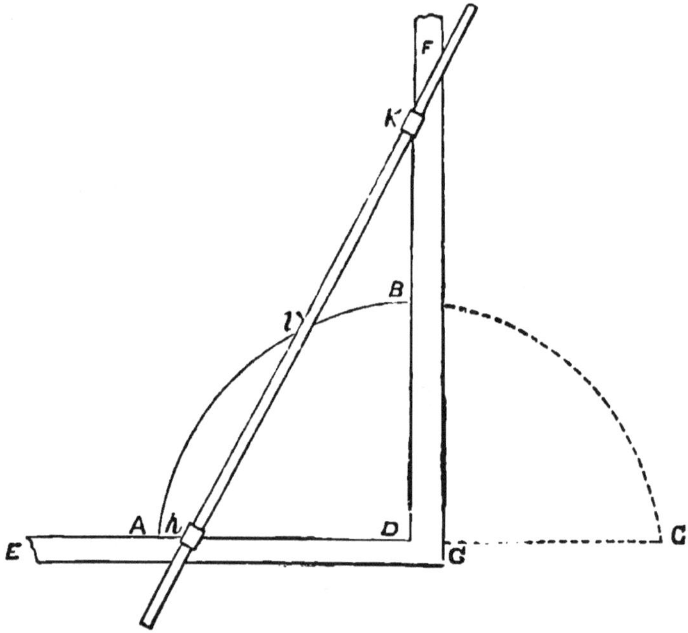

FIG. 29.

Fig. 30 shows a method of describing a parabola by means of a straight rule and a square, its double ordinate and abscissa being given. Let A C be the double ordinate, and D B the abscissa. Bisect D C in F; join B F, and draw F E perpendicular to B F, cutting the axis B D produced in F From B set off B G equal to D E, and G will be the focus of the parabola. Make B L equal to B G, and lay the rule on straight-edge H K on L, and parallel to A C. Take a string, M F G, equal in length to L E ; attach one of its ends to a pin, or other fastening, at G, and its other end to the end M, of the square M N O. If now the square be slid along the straight-edge, and the string be pressed against

its edge M N, a pencil placed in the bight at F will describe
the curve.

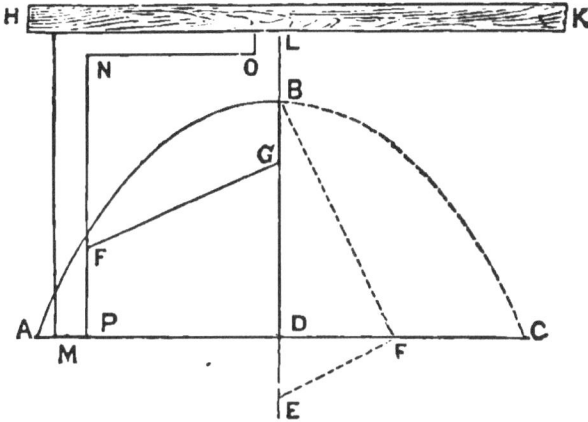

FIG. 30.

The two arms of a horizontal lever are respectively
9 inches and 13 inches in length from the suspending
point; a weight of 10 lbs. is suspended from the shorter
arm, and it is required to know what weight will be required to suspend on the long arm to make it balance.
Set a bevel on the blade of square at 13 inches and the
other end of the bevel on the 9 inch mark on tongue of
square, then slide the bevel from 13 inches to 10 on the
blade of square, and the answer will be found on the
tongue of the square. It is easy to see how this rule can
be reversed so that a weight required for the shorter arm
can be found.

Fig. 31 shows how to get the flare for a hopper 4 feet
across the top and 16 inches perpendicular depth. Add to
the depth one-third of the required size of the discharge

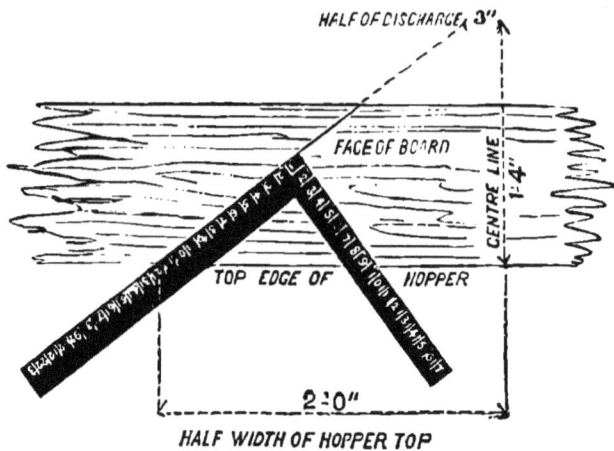

FIG. 31.

hole (the draft represents a 6-inch hole), which makes 18 inches, which is represented on the tongue of the square. (The figures on the draft are 9 and 12, which produce the same bevel.) Then take one-half, 24 inches of the width across the top of the hopper, which is represented on the blade of the square. Than scribe along the blade as represented by the dotted lines, which gives the required flare. (The one-third added to the depth is near enough for all practical purpose for the discharge.)

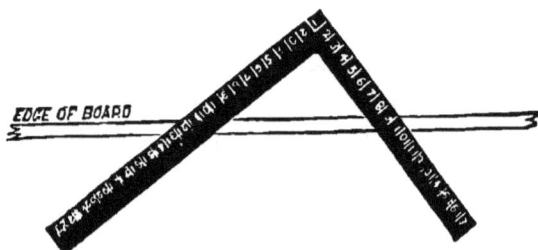

FIG. 32.

Fig. 32 shows how to apply the square to the edge of a board in order to obtain the bevel to form the joint. Using the same figures as in Fig. 31, scribe across the edge of the board by the side of the tongue, as shown by dotted lines. The long point being the outside.

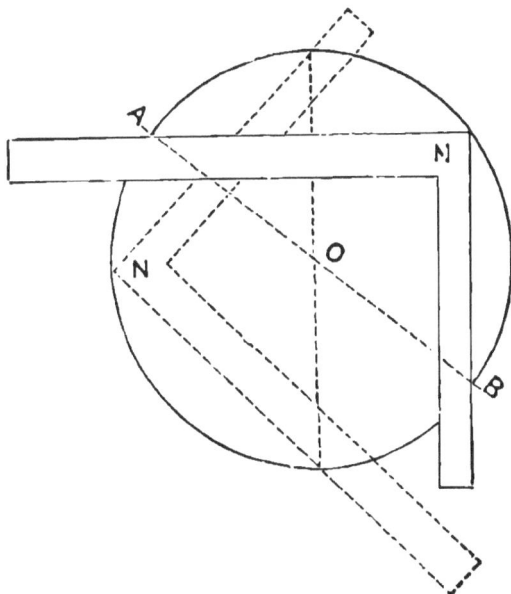

FIG. 33.

On Fig. 33 we show a quick method of finding the centre of a circle: Let N N, the corner of the square, touch the circumference, and where the blade and tongue cross it will be divided equally; then move the square to any other place and mark in the same way and straight edge across, and where the line crosses A, B, as at O, there will be the centre of the circle.

1 and 2, Fig. 34, are taken from Gould's *Wood-Working Guide.*

The portion marked A, exhibits a method of finding the lines for eight-squaring a piece of timber with the square, by placing the block on the piece, and making the points seven inches from the ends of the square, from which to draw the lines for the sides of the octagonal piece required.

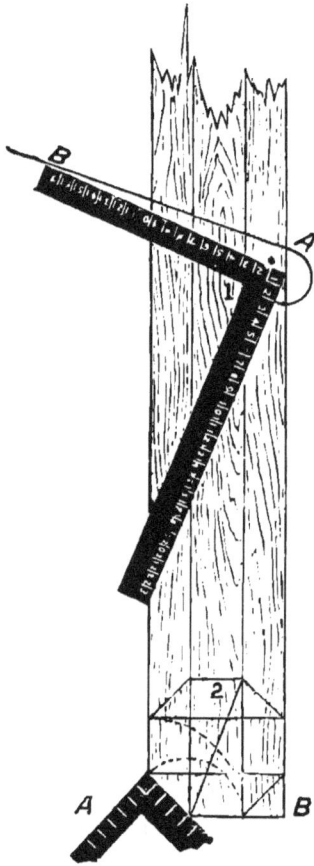

At the heel of the square is shown a method of cutting a board to fit any angle with the square and compass, by placing the square in the angle, and taking the distance from the heel of the square to the angle A, in the compass; then lay the square on the piece to be fitted, with the distance taken, and from the point A, draw the line A B, which will give the angle to cut the piece required.

At 2 is shown a method of constructing a polygonal figure of eight sides; by placing the square on the line A B, with equal distances on the blade and tongue, as shown; the curve lines show the method of transferring the distances; the diagonal gives the intersection at the angles.

Fig. 34.

There are at least a dozen different ways of forming octagonal figures by the square; some of them are tedious
and difficult, while others can not be applied under all cir-
cumstances. The method shown at Fig. 35 is handy and
easily understood.

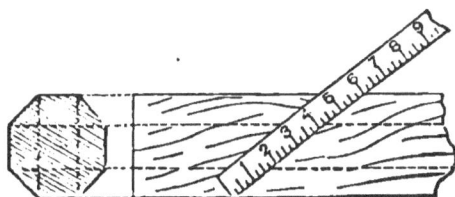

Fig. 35.

An equilateral triangle can be formed by taking half of
one side on the tongue of the square, as shown at Fig. 36.
The line along the edge of the tongue forms the mitre for

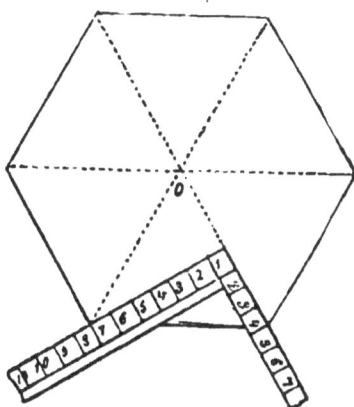

Fig. 36.

the triangle, and the line along the edge of the blade forms
the mitre cut for the joints of a hexagon, and as six equi-

lateral triangles form a hexagon when one point of each is placed at a central point, *o*, it follows that a hexagon may be constructed by the square above.

The following is a good method for obtaining the cuts for a horizontal and raking cornice; it is correct and simple; the gutter to be always cut a square mitre.

The seat or run of the rafter on the blade, R C, Fig. 37, the rise of the roof on the tongue, A C, mark against the tongue, gives the cut for the side of the box, A C. The

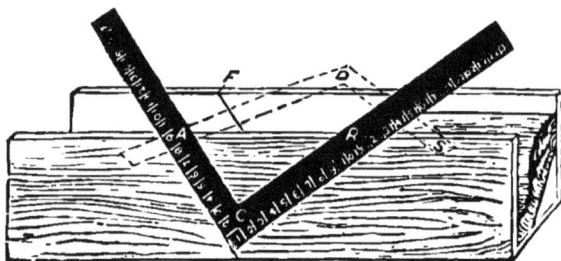

Fig. 37.

diagonal A, R, which is the length of the rafter on the blade A, D, the seat of the rafter on the tongue D, S, mark against the blade gives the cut across the box, A D.   D A C is the mitre cut to fit the gutter; then if we square across the box from A, it gives F, A, C the cut for the gable peak.

At Fig. 38 is shown a method for obtaining either the butt or mitre cuts, for "Hopper" work.

The line, s s, in the cut represents the edge of a board; the line, A B, the flare of hopper. Lay the square on the face of the board so that the blade will coincide with flare of hopper, A B, then mark by the tongue the line B C, then square from edge of board, s s, cutting the angle B.

Now we have a figure that will, when used on the steel

square, give the cuts for a hopper of any flare, either with butt or mitre joints.

To find bevel to cut across face of board:

Take A B on blade and A D on tongue, bevel of tongue is the bevel required.

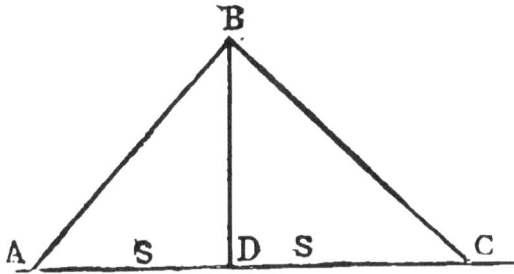

Fig. 38.

To find the bevel for butt-joint: Take B C on blade and A D on tongue; bevel of tongue is the bevel required.

To find the bevel for mitre joint: Take B C on blade and D C on tongue; bevel of tongue is the bevel required.

It will be seen that this is a very simple method of solving what is usually considered a very difficult problem.

PART II.

The following useful applications of the square were kindly furnished for this work, by Mr. Croker; several of them are new and original:

Consider the blade of the square as representing the *span* of a building, but without any reference to actual or scale measurement. Next, some particular portion of the blade is to be taken as the rise of the *supposed* building; if a third, fourth, or half pitch is required, then a third, fourth, or a half of the blade is conceived as the rise which with half the blade solves the pitch. From this it will be seen that half the blade is always taken as the base of the *theoretical common rafter*. Where we have to deal with irregular pitches—by which is meant those pitches which are not a quarter, sixth, third, half, etc., of the building—then the square is to be applied to the irregular pitch with the blade lying in the direction of the pitch and the centre of the blade at the intersection of pitch and base line of the common rafter, and the resulting distance on the tongue, where it intersects the base line, is the distance to be taken as the rise of the theoretical rafter. Let us now take a hip-roof over a square plan (for all the rules apply only to square planned building), and the practical problems supposed to need solution are: Length of common rafters, the plumb and level cuts; length of hip-rafter, its plumb and level cuts; bevel of jacks and sheeting boards against the hips; "backing" of the hip-rafter, top and down bevel of a purlin mitering against the hip with its surface in line with the plane of the roof. If the student can readily and intelligently solve these problems, he will be in a position to make extensions in the principles involved. Let the width of building under consideration be 24 feet wide, and of one third pitch.

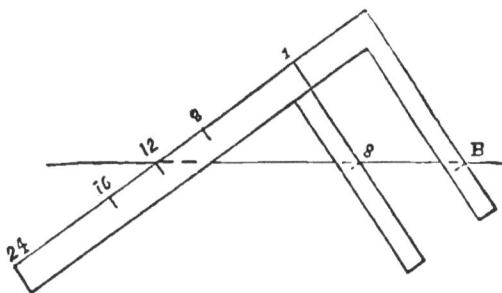

FIG. 36.

Let 1, 12, Fig. 36, be the base of the theoretical common rafter, eight inches rise, equal to one third of the blade, because it is a third pitch; mark along the blade and extend the heel, making it and 12 equal to half the width of the actual building to a scale of 1½ inch to a foot; this is a much better scale to work by than an inch one, being larger and more legible, eighths being inches, sixteenths, ½ inches, etc., thus enabling very accurate measurements to be taken. By the way, it is a good plan to have the square stamped off on the eighths side at every 1½ inches for feet, for more readily counting the scale; then mark along the tongue at B, which gives B 12 the length of common rafter; level cut on blade and plumb cut on tongue. Next take the rise of the theoretical common rafter on the tongue, and 17 inches

on the blade, as the theoretical base of the hip-rafter;
place the square as shown at Fig. 37; then multiply the

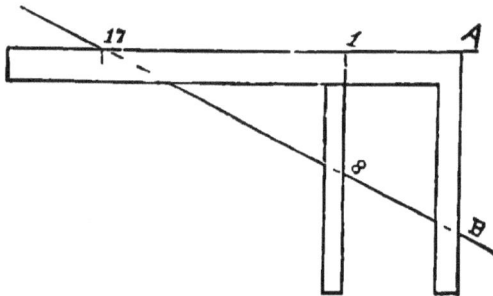

FIG. 37.

actual base of common rafter 12, (Fig. 36.) by 1·414 =
16·968 feet, or 17 feet, practically, which set off on blade at A
17; mark on tongue at B, then B 17 is the length of hip-
rafter.   For the bevels of jacks and sheeting-boards against
hips take the diagonal B 12—theoretical rafter—Fig. 36, on
the blade with half the blade—the theoretical base—and
place the square as shown at Fig. 38, then mark along the
blade for bevel of jacks, and along tongue for bevel of
sheeting-boards.

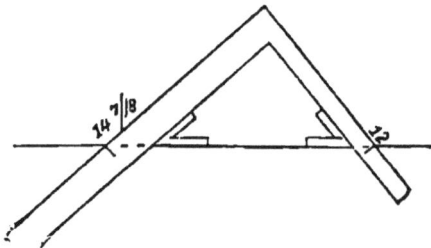

FIG. 38,

For the "backing" of hip, take the diagonal of the theoretical hip-rafter, 8, 17 (Fig 37), on the blade, and its rise—8 inches—on the tongue, and place square as shown at Fig. 39; mark by the tongue which gives the bevel re-

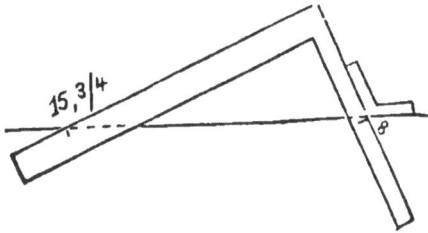

FIG. 39.

quired.   To get the upper bevel of a purlin lying in the plane of the roof, take the bevel at tongue (Fig. 38), for the down bevel take the blade distance 14·7—16 (Fig. 38) on the blade with the theoretical rise—8 ; place the square as shown at Fig. 40 ; mark by the tongue which gives the bevel required.

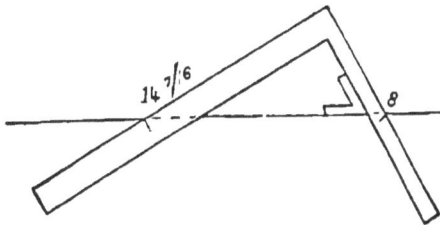

FIG. 40.

Fig. 41 shows how any length or breadth within the extent of the blade of the square can be instantly divided into any equal parts.   Let A and B represent the edges of a board, say 8¾ inches, wide, to be divided into 5 equal parts ; take any

convenient 5 parts, say 15 inches, because $5 \times 3 = 15$, placing
heel of square fair to edge B, and 15 to edge A; mark off at
every 3 inches on blade, as shown, and draw lines through
these points, which will divide the board as required. We
will here show how the square can be used to solve problems
in proportion; for instance, if 1500 feet of boards cost
$10.75, what will 600 feet cost? Take 15 on the blade

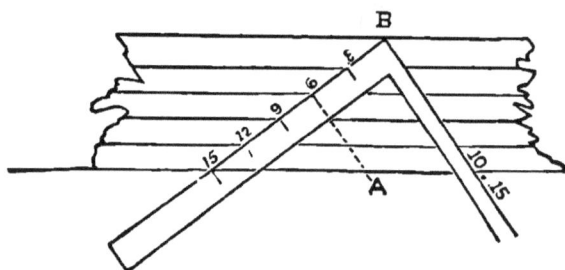

FIG. 41.

and 10·75 on the tongue, and place the square as shown at
Fig. 41, then count from 15 towards B, and from this point
draw parallel to tongue; 6 A, this is the answer required.

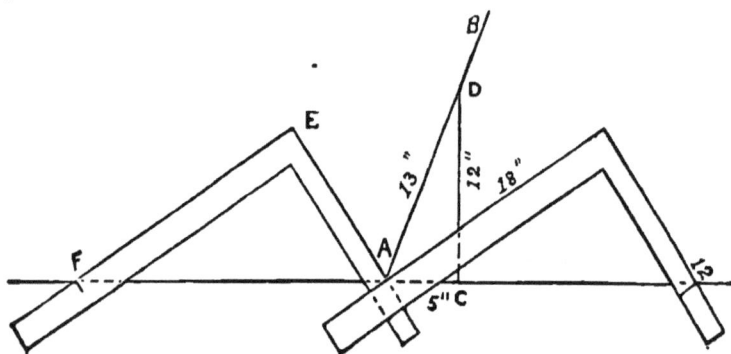

FIG. 42.   FIG. 43.

Figs. 42 and 43 show quite a novel and useful way of bisecting any angle. Let A 12, A B be the given sides of an acute angle to be bisected. At any convenient point as C square C D from C 12. Now take C D on the tongue, and the sum of A D and A C on the blade of the square, place as shown in the Figure, then mark by the blade, which is the bisection required. If the angle is obtuse, as A B, A F, (Fig. 42), produce a convenient distance, as A C, square over C D, take C D on the tongue, and the sum of A D, A C, on the blade, place square as shown, and mark by the tongue for the required bisection.

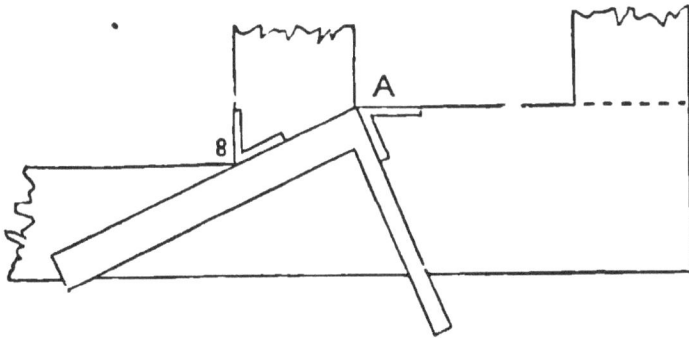

FIG. 44.

Fig. 44 shows a handy way of finding the bevel of rails to diminish door stiles. Place the square fair with the known joint A B, mark by the tongue, then the resulting bevel at A is the same as that at B.

PART III.

The following rules have been gathered from various sources, chiefly, however. from papers recently published in the *Scientific American Supplement*, by John O. Connell, of St. Louis, and from papers contributed to the *Builder and Wood-Worker*, by Wm. E. Hill, of Terre Haute, Ind.

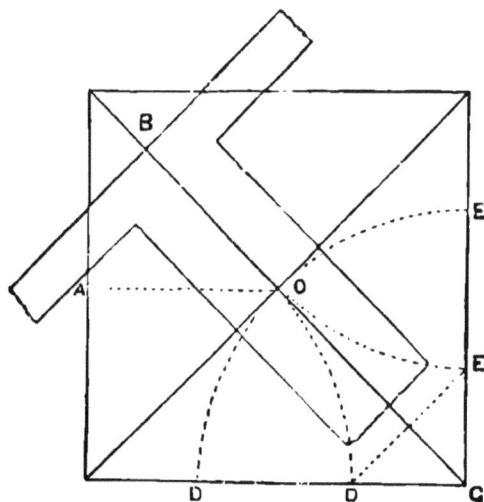

FIG. 45

* Fig. 45 shows how an octagon can be produced by the aid of a steel square. Prick off the distance A O equal to half the distance of the square; mark this distance on the blade of the square from B to O, place the square on the

diagonal, as shown, and square over each way. Do the same at every angle, and the octagon is complete.

To obtain the same figure with the compasses, proceed as follows : Take half the diagonal on the compasses, make a little over a quarter sweep from c, and at the insersection at D and c, then D and c form one side of an octagonal figure.

Again: take a piece of timber twelve inches square, as at Fig. 46 ; take twelve inches on the blade and tongue from A to B, and A to c, mark at the point A, operate similarly on the opposite edge, and the marked points will be guides for guage-lines for the angles forming an octagon. The remaining three sides of the timber can be treated in the same manner.

These points can be found with a carpenter's rule as follows: Lay the

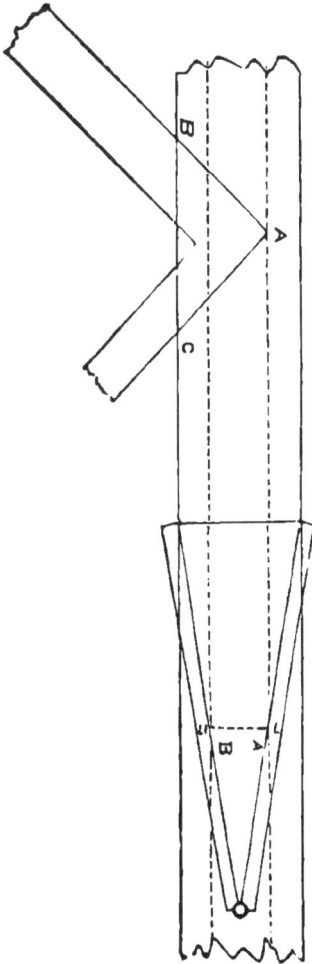

Fig. 46.

rule on the timber, partly opened, as shown, in the cut,
"prick off" at the figures 7 and 17 as at A and B, and
these points will be the guides for the gauge-lines. The
same points can be found by laying the square diagonally
across the timber and " pricking " off 7 and 17.

To make a moulder's flask octagonal proceed as follows :
The flask to be four feet across. Multiply 4×5 (as an
octagon is always as 5 to 12 nearly), which gives 20 ; divide by 12, which gives $1\frac{2}{3}$ feet, cut mitre to suit this
measurement, nail into corners of square box, and you have
an octagon flask at once.

Another method of constructing an octagon is shown at
Fig. 47. Take the side as $a\ b$ for a radius, describe an arc

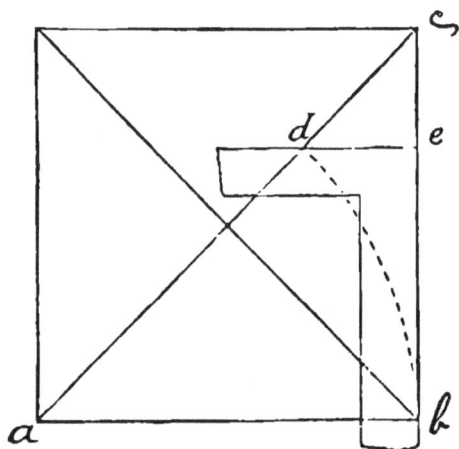

Fig. 47.

cutting the diagonal at d; square over from d to e, and
the point e will then be the gauge-guide for all the sides.

Another method (Fig. 48) is to draw a straight line, *c b*, any length; then let *a b* and *a c* be corresponding figures on the blade and tongue of the square, mark along either and measure the distance of required octagon; move

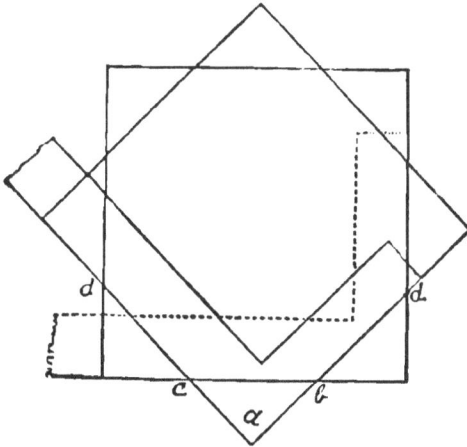

FIG. 48.

the square and mark also. Now use the square the same as before, and the marks *c b* and *b d* are the poin s required.

Fig. 49 shows the application of a long bevel to a square, by which some calculations can be made with greater ease and quickness than by the usual arithmetical process. The largest size of carpenter's bevel placed under the framing square will answer in nearly every case. One edge of each blade should be perfectly straight and the edge of L should be cut out in several places to see the blade E, when placed under the square. The two blades should be fastened together by a thumb-screw. There

should be three holes in L, one near each end and one in
the middle, and a notch filed by each hole, so that the
blade E, may be shifted when necessary.

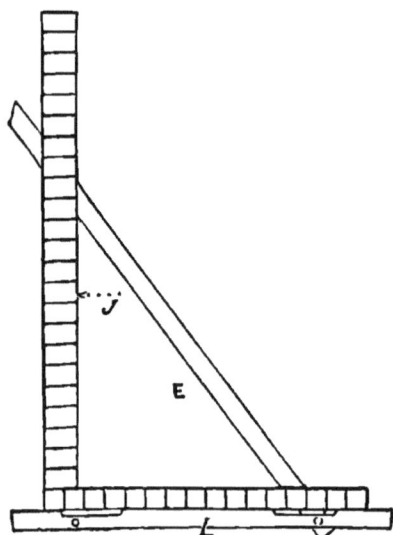

*To Find the Diagonal of a Square by this instrument, set
the blade E to $8\frac{3}{4}$ inches on the tongue and $12\frac{3}{8}$ inches
on the blade.   Then screw the bevel fast; and supposing
the side of the square in question is 11 inches, move blade
E to the 11 inch mark on the tongue, keeping blade L
against the square, when blade E will touch 15 9-16 inches
on the blade, which is the required diagonal.   There is no
special reason for using $8\frac{3}{4}$ and $12\frac{3}{8}$; other numbers may
be employed provided the proportion of 70 to 99 exists
between them.   In the problem just solved as in all that
follow, the bevel being once set to solve a particular ques-

*J. O. Connell.

tion will solve all the others of the same kind, till the bevel
is altered.

Polygons Inscribed in Circles.

Polygons Inscribed in Circles.—In the following table, set
the bevel to the pair of numbers under the polygon to be
inscribed.

No. of sides.	3	4	5	6	7	8	9	10	11	12
Radius........	56	70	74	Side equal to radius.	60	98	22	89	80	85
Side..........	97	99	87		52	75	15	55	45	44

If we require the radius of a circle which will circumscribe an octagon 8 inches on a side, we refer to column 8,
take 98 parts on the blade and 75 on tongue, and
tighten the bevel. As the side of a hexagon equals the
radius of its circle, the side of an octagon must be less than
the radius; hence we shift to 8 inches, that end of the bevel
blade which gives the lesser number, in this case, on the
tongue of the square, as the 75 parts to which the bevel
was set are less than the 98. The required radius is then
indicated on the blade.

We will now explain the figures used in stepping round
a circle forming inscribed polygons from three to twelve
sides: Set bevel or fence to 12 on blade, and the number
opposite each polygon on tongue; move to diameter of
circle; answer of the side of polygon on tongue.

Names.	No. of Sides.	Gauge Points.
Triangle....................................	3	10·40
Square	4	8·49
Pentagon...................................	5	7·05
Hexagon	6	6·00
Heptagon...................................	7	5·21
Octagon....................................	8	4·60
Nonagon	9	4·11
Decagon....................................	10	3·71
Undecagon	11	3·39
Dodecagon..................................	12	3·11

To divide a circle into a given number of parts, multiply the corresponding number in column one and the product is the chord to lay off on circumference.   The side of a polygon is known, to find the radius of a circle that will circumscribe :   Multiply the given side by the corresponding number opposite of polygon in column two.

No. of Sides.	Name of Polygon.	Angle.	Angle of Polygon.	Column 1.	Column 2.
3	Triangle 120		60	1·732	·5773
4	Square. 90		90	1·414	·7071
5	Pentagon 72		108	1·775	·8510
6	Hexagon.............. 60		120	Radius.	Side.
7	Heptagon............. 51 3·7		128 4·7	·8677	1·152
8	Octagon 45		135	·7653	1·3071
9	Nonagon 40		140	·6840	1·4863
10	Decagon 36		144	·6180	1·6181
11	Undecagon............ 32 8·11		147 3·11	·5634	1·7754
12	Dodecagon............ 30		150	·5176	1·9323

The side of a polygon is known, to find the length of perpendicular :   Set bevel or fence to the tabulated numbers below.   Example :   The side of an octagon is 12, set bevel to 23 on tongue, 27 11-16 on blade.   Blade gives the answer.

No. of Sides.	3	4	5	6	7	8	9	10	11	12
Perpendicular..	9	1	30	13	27 3·4	27 7·10	50 3·4	28 1·2	31 3·4	26
Side of Polygon	31 1·5	2	35 1·4	15	26	23	37	18 1·2	30 1·2	14

To Inscribe three Equal Circles in a circle of given diameter.   Set to 6½ on tongue and 14 on blade.   Move the bevel to the given diameter on the blade and the required diameter appears on the tongue.

Four equal circles require a bevel of 2·91 and 14.

The following also, is another use for the square and bevel combined.

If a person is drawing a machine on a scale of 1½ inch to the foot, he may simply lay a common rule under the square, touching the 12 inch mark on the blade, and the 1½ inch mark on the tongue; he then possesses a contrivance by which he may easily reduce from one scale to the other. For instance, if a piece of stick 2¾ inches square is to go into the construction, the draughtsman finds the 9¼ inch mark on the blade, that is 2¾ inches back from the 12 inch mark, and measures square out to the rule. This distance is the reduced section of ·the stick. A straight mark, drawn on a table or a drawing board, serves as well as a rule.

Conveyors' shaft 5 inches in diameter, 12 feet long, pitch of flights 9 inches; make a posteboard template; multiplying the diameter by 3·1416 gives the base, and the 9 is the altitude. The paper would be 9 inches altitude, 15 71-100 base; draw a line along shaft, place altitude or 9 inches along this line, scribe along the hypothenuse; this gives the spiral course of flight. This principle also teaches how to cut round sticks of straight timber by marking along base of template. take square on each end the same as taking a stick out of wind, before striking lines.

The cuts for the edges of the pieces of a hexagonal hopper are found by subtracting the width of one piece at the bottom, viz., the width of same at top, and taking the remainder on the tongue, and depth of side on blade. The tongue gives the cut. For the cut on the face of the sides, take 7-12 of the rise on the tongue, and the depth of side on the blade. The tongue gives the cut. The bevel for the top and bottom edges is found by taking the rise on the blade, and the run on the tongue; the latter gives the cut.

To find the cut of an octagonal hopper for the face of

the board and also the edge, substract the rise from the width of side ; take the remainder on the tongue and width of side on blade; the tongue gives the cut. The edge of the stuff is to be square when applying the bevel. The bevel for the top and bottom edges of the sides is found by taking the rise on the blade, and run on the tongue, the latter gives the cut. This makes the edges horizonatal. The edges are not to be beveled till the four sides are cut.

Tc lay off Angles of 60° and 30°.—Mark any number of inches, say 14, on an indefinite line. Place the blade against one extremity of this distance, and the 7 inch mark of the tongue at the other. The tongue then forms an angle of 60° with the indefinite line, and the blade an angle of 30°.

To Find the Bevels and Width of Sides and Ends of a Square Hopper.—Fig. 50. The large square represents the upper edges of the hopper and the small one the lower edges, or base. The width of the sides and ends is found in this way: Take the run a b on the tongue, and the perpendicular height a d on the blade. It is thus found in the same manner as the length of a brace. To find the cut for a butt joint, take width of side on blade and half the length of the base on tongue; the latter gives the cut. For a mitre joint take width of side on the blade and perpendicular height on tongue ; the latter gives the cut.

For the cut across the sides of the boards, take the run

a b on the tongue, and the width of side on blade; the tongue gives the cut. The inside corners of the sides and ends are longer than the outside, so if a hopper is to be of

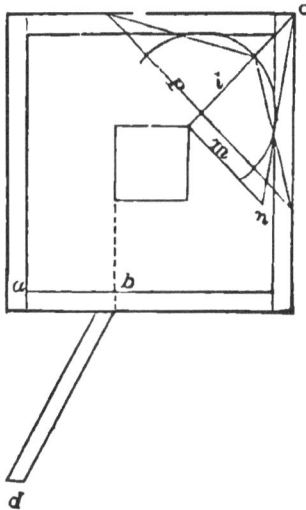

FIG. 50.

a certain size, the lengths of ends and sides are to be measured on the inside edge of each piece, and the bevels struck across the edges to these marks. This is only in case of butt joints. Of course if the hopper is to be square, the thickness of the sides must be taken from the ends.

If the top and bottom edges are to be horizontal, the bevel is thus found : Take the perpendicular height of hopper on the blade and the run on the tongue, the latter gives both cuts. A hopper can be made by the above method by getting the outside dimensions at top and bottom, and the perpendicular height.

In large hoppers pieces are put down along the corners

to strengthen them. The length, and the bevel to fit the corner are thus found : Suppose the top of hopper is 8 feet, and the bottom 18 inches square. Find the diagonals of each, subtract the one from the other, and half the remainder is the run for the corner piece. From the length of this run, l, and the rise, $a\,b$, we find the length of the corner piece. To find the bevel or backing, take on the blade the length of the corner piece and on the tongue the rise; the latter gives the bevel. Another method is to draw the line, l, to represent the seat of the corner piece, set off square with this the line m, of the same length as the run, $a\,b$. Then draw $n\,o$, which is the length of the corner piece. To find the backing, draw a line, p, anywhere across l, at right angles therewith, and at its intersection with line, l, strike a circle tangent to $n\,o$. From the point of intersection of the circle with l, draw lines to the extremities of p. The angle made by these lines is the bevel or backing.

Another method generally employed for finding the bevels of hoppers is to bevel the top and bottom edges of the sides and ends to the angle they are to stand at, then to lay a bevel set to a mitre, or angle of $45°$, on the beveled edge, and that will lay off a mitre joint, while a try-square will lay off a butt joint. An angle of $45°$ will mitre only those boxes with sides which are vertical and square with each other.

When the sides and ends of a rectangular box or hopper are of the same width, that is, when sides and ends slope at equal angles, the bevels, either butt or mitre, are found as for square hoppers.

When a hopper has the sides and ends of different widths, that is, when sides and ends stand at different angles, both having the same rise, find the cuts for each from its respective rise, run and width.

Roofing.—Fig. 51. A hip-roof with two corners out of square is given an example, the dimensions of which are: width 15 feet, rise of roof 5 feet, length 30 feet on the

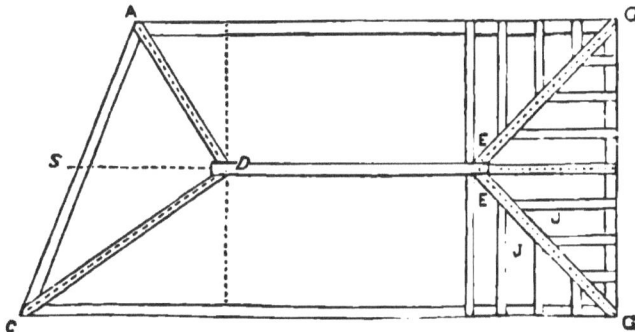

FIG. 51.

shorter side, 33 feet on the longer. The timbers A D, C D, E G, E G, are the hip rafters; J J the jack rafters. The seats of each hip rafter should form a square, so that each pair of jack rafters, J J, for instance, may be cut of equal length.

Lengths and Bevels of Hip-Rafters.—We will first consider those on the square end of the roof. In order to find their length, it is first necessary to obtain their run, which is found as follows: Take half the width of building on both blade and tongue, whence is obtained the length of seat from G to E, at the intersection of the dotted lines. By similar use of the square, this length with the rise of roof, gives the length of the hip-rafter. The lengths of all the rafters

should be measured along the middle, as the dotted lines
show.   This is the full length; half the thickness of the
ridge-pole is to be taken off, measured square back from
the bevel.

The bevel of the upper end of a hip-rafter is called the
down bevel.   It is always square with the lower end bevel,
hence these bevels are found by the parts taken on the
square to find the lengths of the hip-rafters.   Another
method is to take 17 inches on the blade and the number
of inches of rise to the foot, that is, the rise in inches divided by half the width of roof in feet—on the tongue.   The
tongue gives the down bevel, the blade the lower end bevel.
The reason for the foregoing is that when the hip-rafters are
square with each other, the seat of the hip is the diagonal
of a square whose side is half the width of building.   The
diagonal of a square with a 12 inch side is 17 inches nearly.
So if the rise of roof in 1 foot is 6 inches, the rise of hip-
rafter will be that only in 17 inches.   The directions here
given assume that the hip-rafter abuts the ridge-pole at right
angles, but as the ground plan of the roof shows that they
meet at an acute angle, another bevel must be considered,
called the side bevel of the hip-rafters.   Were there no slope
to the roof, the bevel where they meet the ridge pole would
be an angle of 45°, as the hips would be square with each
other.   When a pitch or slope is given, the hips depart from
the right angle, and therefore the side bevels are always
less than 45°.   Take the length of hip on the blade, and
its run on the tongue; the blade gives the cut.

Backing of the hip-rafters.   The backs of the hip-rafters
must be beveled to lie even with the planes of the roof.
This bevel must slope from the middle toward either side.

It is found by taking the length of hip on blade, and the
rise of the roof on tongue. The latter gives the bevel.

To find the lengths of the jack-rafters: Suppose there
are to be four between the corner and the first common
rafter; then there are five spaces, which, by dividing 7 foot
6 inches by 5, are 1 foot 2 inches from centre to centre of
jacks. The rise of roof, also divided by 5, gives 1 foot rise
for the shortest rafter. The run is 1 foot 6 inches; as both
rise and run are given, the length down and lower bevels
are found therefrom. The next jack has double the
rise, run and length of the first; the following one three
times, and the fourth four times. All the measurements
are to proceed on or from the middle lines of the jacks.

The side bevel of all the jack-rafters is obtained by taking
the length of a common rafter on the blade and its run on
the tongue; the bevel on the blade gives the result.

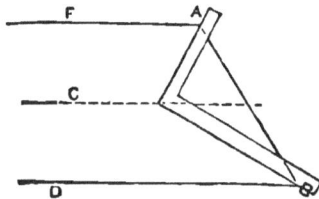

FIG. 52.

Let us now consider the end of the building out of square.
Fig. 52 illustrates the method of laying down the seats of
the hips. To find the lengths of these hips, the lengths of
the seats must be got by taking half the width of building
on blade, and the distance from the end of the dotted line
crossing the roof, to the corner on the tongue. The length

of the seat so obtained taken on the square, with the rise of the roof, gives the length of the respective hip-rafter.

The down and lower end bevels are found as in the previous hip-rafters. To obtain each side bevel, add the distance from the dotted line to the corner and the gain of the hip-rafter; take the sum on the blade, and half the width of building on the tongue; the latter gives the cut.

The lengths, etc., of the jack-rafters on the side, are determined as at the square end of the roof; the side bevel being found by taking the length of a common rafter on the blade, and the distance from the dotted line to corner on the tongue. The latter showing the bevel.

The lengths of jack-rafters on the end. Assuming there are to be four jacks between the corner and the centre included, half the length of the end of the roof must be divided by 5. One side of the roof being 3 feet longer than the other, we place 3 feet, on tongue, and 15 feet, the width of building, on the blade, and thus obtain the distance from corner to corner on the end of the roof. Half this divided by 5 gives the distance of the jacks apart. The distance from where the middle lines of the hips meet to the middle point of the end of the roof is also to be divided by 5, the quotient giving the run of the shortest rafter. The rise is the same as for the jacks on the square end.

These rules give the full length of rafter, so that when hips come against a ridge-pole or jacks against a hip, half the thickness of pole or hip, squared back from their down bevels, must be taken off.

Side bevels of these jacks are obtained by adding the distance from the dotted line to the corner to the gain of a common rafter in running that distance; take this on the blade, and half the width of building on the tongue. The blade gives the bevel.

Trusses.—Fig. 53. A is the straining beam, B the brace, T the tie beam. Generally the brace has about one-third the length of tie beam for a run. From the rise and run find the length and lower end bevel of the brace. After marking the lower end bevel on the stick, add to it just what is cut out of the tie beam. The bevel of the upper end of the brace where it butts against the straining beam is found in the following manner. Take the length of the

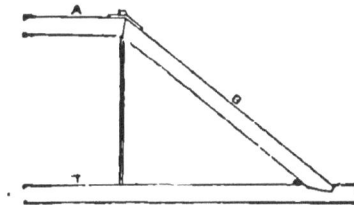

FIG. 53.

brace, or a proportional part, and mark it on the edge of a board; take half the rise of the brace on the tongue, lay it to one of these marks on the board, and move the blade till it touches the other mark on board. A line drawn along the tongue gives the bevel for both brace and straining beam. The angle made between brace and straining beam is thus bisected. Lay off the measurements from the outside of the timbers. Put a bolt where shown, with a washer under the head to fit the angle of straining beam and brace,

There are quite a number of methods of obtaining approximate proportions of the diameter of circles to their circumferences. The true proportion, or, as it is sometimes expressed, "the squaring of the circle," is one of those feats, like the discovery of "perpetual motion," and is as far from being accomplished now as ever. At any rate, it makes but little difference at this time, to the operative mechanic, whether the circle can be squared or not, so long as he can get near enough to the truth to satisfy the requirements at hand satisfactorily; and to aid him in this, the following method is shown of obtaining the circumferences of circles when the diameter is given, by use of the square. Of course, as shown in the cut, the rule will apply to circles of any reasonable dimensions.

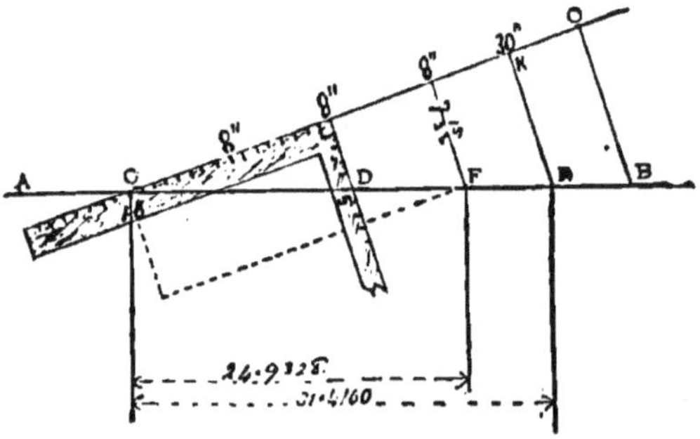

Fig. 54.

Let A B, Fig. 54, be a straight line, or the straight edge of a board; then apply the square as shown, placing the 16-inch mark on the blade at C, and the 5-inch mark on the tongue at D. See that the junctions of the blade and tongue of the square with the line A B, are accurately placed, for on this depends the truth of the results. Now, suppose we wish to ascertain the circumference of a circle

whose diameter is 8 inches; commencing at the point, C,
we space off the diameter, 8 inches, three times, on the line
C O, as shown at 8" 8" 8"; then square down the line 8" F,
then C F will be the circumference of a circle whose diameter is 8. It will be seen, by dotted lines in the cut, that
the circumference equals the diagonal of a rectangle whose
sides are respectively 24 and 7½⅖ inches; so that by adopt-
ing these figures (24 and 7½⅖) it enables the operative to
use the full length and capacity of the square. The
better way, however, is to work from a basis of 16 and 5,
and draw the lines, C O and A B, to considerable length, so
that they may be made available for dimensions beyond
the range of the square. Now, let us suppose an instance
where the circumference of a circle is wanted, whose diameter is 10; we simply space off three tens, or thirty inches,
on the line C O, which, in this case, is at K. Square down
from K to R, and C R is the length sought.

Now, to prove this, let us proceed as follows: Diam. =
10 × 3·1416 = 31·4160, or nearly thirty-one inches and
fifteen thirty-seconds of an inch. Now, if we measure C R,
we will find that the distance is exactly 31·4160 inches,
and is, therefore, the answer sought. It will be seen by
these examples that the circumferences of circles may be
easily obtained when the diameters are known. So, also,
may the diameters be found when the circumferences are
known, for by laying off the circumference on the line A B,
as C D in Fig. 54, for instance, and then applying the
square as there exhibited, and dividing the distance from
the heel of the square to the point C into three equal parts.
One of these parts is the diameter of the circle whose circumference equals the distance from C to D.

In my experience, I have frequently been asked how a mitre, or equal joint, could be laid off by using the square.

The matter is so simple, that it was thought unnecessary to insert it in the first edition, but the many inquiries on the subject that have been received since the work was published, induces me to give a few examples of the manner in which advanced workmen generally accomplish this end. Let Fig. 55 represent an oblique angle formed

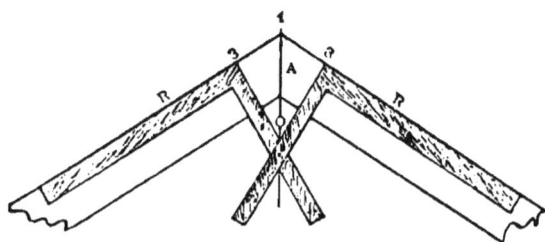

FIG. 55.

by two parallel boards. To obtain the joint, A, space off equal distances from the point 1 to 3, 3, then square over from the lines, R, R, keeping the heel of the square at the points, 3, 3. At the junction of the lines formed by the tongue of the square at o will be one point, and 1 will be the other by which the joint line, A, is defined.

To find the line of juncture for an acute angle, we proceed as follows: Fig. 56 represents two parallel boards; 1 the extreme angle, 3, 3 equal distances from the angle 1 and are the points where the heel of the square must rest to form the lines o, 3; o shows the junction of the lines formed by the blade of the square. Draw a line from o to 1, and the line, A, formed, is the bevel required.

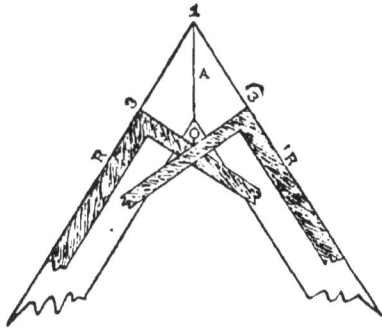

FIG. 56.

It will be seen, by these two examples, that the bevel of
a junction at any angle may be obtained by this method.

Sometimes, when estimating on work, it becomes necessary to get the length of braces and other timbers, that
would require considerable figuring to obtain if the usual

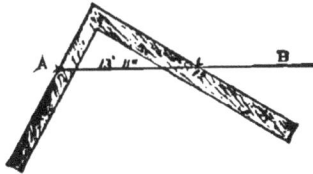

FIG. 57.

method of finding the length of the third side of a right-
angled triangle was adopted. The square, at this juncture,
may be made use of with advantage, where the length of
the lines wanted is within the range of the instrument, and
almost any dimensions may be manipulated, by making the
subdivisions of the inch represent inches, feet, or yards.
Suppose we want to get the length of a brace with unequal
run of 7 and 12 feet respectively. Lay the two-foot rule

across the square, putting the end on 7 on the tongue, and
cutting the 12-inch line on the blade; then, as shown in
Fig. 57, we will have on the side of the rule A B, 13 feet
11 inches, or say 14 feet, which is near enough for the
estimator's purpose, and if required for working purposes,
the exact length and bevels may be obtained by careful
measurement.

Conclusion.—The ingenious and intelligent workman,
after thoroughly mastering the foregoing applications of the
" Steel Square," will awaken to the fact that the tool may
be used for the solution of a thousand and one little
matters that will crop up in his every-day calling, and by
a combination or adaptation of the rules presented, he will
be able to overcome all ordinary difficulties in obtaining
cuts, bevels, and lines for roofs, hoppers, mouldings, etc.

PART IV.

Miscellaneous Rules and Memoranda.—The practical carpenter and joiner will frequently want to use the more elaborate methods of obtaining solutions where the problems are complicated and various; and the following rules are inserted in this work with a view of reaching *some* of the problems that appear to be beyond the range of the Steel Square without making such intricate combinations as would be sure to lead to confusion in ordinary hands.

Hip-Roofs.—The principles to be determined in a hip-roof are seven; namely:

1st. The angle which a common rafter makes with the level of the top of the building; that is, the pitch of the roof.

2nd. The angle which the hip-rafter makes with the level of the building.

3d. The angles which the hip-rafter makes with the adjoining sides of the roof. This is called the backing of the hip.

4th. The height of the roof, or the "rise," as it is called.

5th. The lengths of the common rafters.

6th. The lengths of the hip-rafters.

7th. The distance between the centre line of the hip-rafter and the centre line of the first entire common rafter.

The first, fourth, fifth and seventh are generally given, and from these the others may be found, as will be shown by the following illustrations: Let A B C D Fig. 58, be the plan of a roof. Draw G H parallel to the sides, A D, B C, and in the middle of the distance between them. From the points A, B, C, D, with any radius, describe the curves *a b*, *a b*, cutting the sides of the plan at *a*, *b*. From these points, with any radius, bisect the fou angles of the plan at *r*, *r*, *r*, *r*, and from A, B, C, D, through the points,

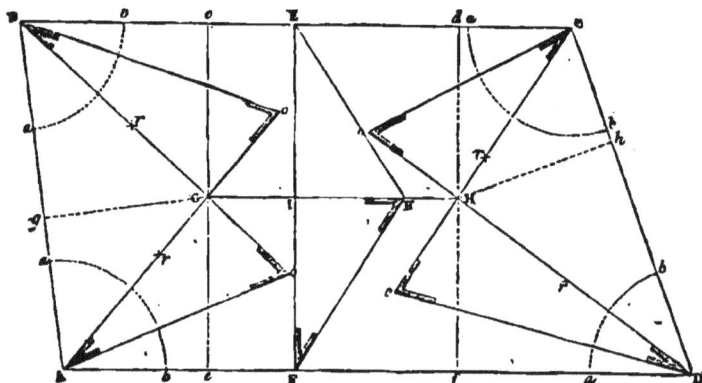

FIG. 58.

r, *r*, *r*, *r*, draw the lines of the hip-rafters, A G, B G, C H, D H, cutting the ridge-line, G H, in G and H, and produce them indefinitely. The dotted lines, *c c*, *d f*, are the seats of the last entire common rafters. Through any point in the ridge-line, I, draw E I F at right angles to G H. Make I K equal to the height or rise of roof, and join E K, F K; then E K is the length of a common rafter. Make G *o*, H *o*, equal to I K, the rise of the roof, and join A *o*, B *o*, C *o*, D *o*, for the length of the hip-rafters. If the triangles, A *o* G, B *o* G, be turned round their seats, A G, B G, until their perpendiculars are perpendicular to the plane of the plan, the points, o o, and the lines, G *o*, G *o*, will coincide, and the rafters, A *o*, B *o*, be in their true positions.

If the roof is irregular, and it is required to keep the
ridge level, we proceed as shown in Fig. 59.

Bisect the angles of two ends by the lines A b, B b, C G,
D G, in the same manner as in Fig. 58; and through G
draw the lines G E, G F, parallel to the sides, C B, D A, re-

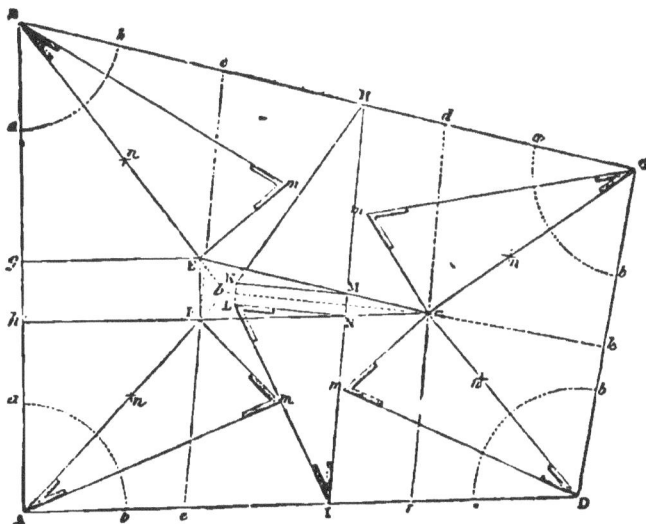

FIG. 59.

spectively cutting A b, B b, in E and F; join E F; then the
triangle, E G F, is a flat, and the remaining triangle and
trapeziums are the inclined sides. Join G b, and draw H I
perpendicular to it; at the points M and N, where H I cuts
the lines G E, G F, draw M K, N L perpendicular to H I, and
make them equal to the rise; then draw H K, I L for the
lengths of the common rafters. At E, set up E m perpendicular to B E; make it equal to M K or N L, and join B m
for the length of the hip-rafter, and proceed in the same
manner to obtain A m, C m, D m.

To find the backing of a hip-rafter, when the plan is

right-angled, we proceed as shown in Fig. 60. Let B *b*, *b* C
be the common rafters, A D the width of the roof, and A B
equal to one-half the width.   Bisect B C in *a*, and join A *a*,
D *a*.   From *a* set off *a c*, *a d* equal to the height of the

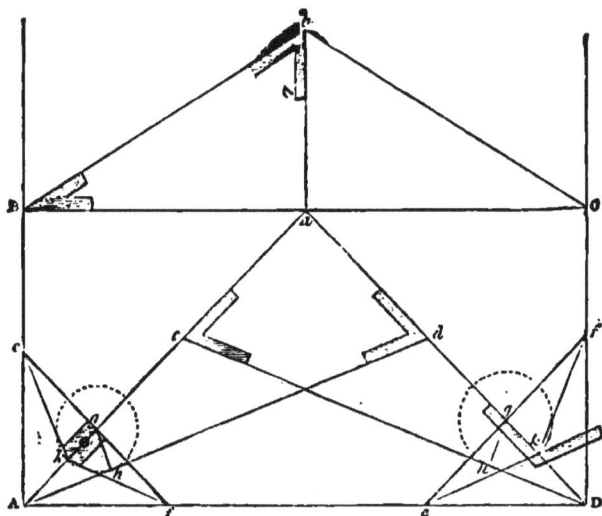

FIG. 60.

roof *a b*, and join A *d*, D *c*; then A *d*, D *c* are the hip-
rafters. To find the backing: from any point *h* in A *d*,
draw the perpendicular *h g*, cutting A *a* in *g*; and through
g draw perpendicular to A *a* the line *e f*, cutting A B, A D
in *e* and *f*. Make *g k* equal to *g h*, and join *k e*, *k f*: the
angle *e k f* is the angle of the backing of the hip-rafter C.

Fig. 61 shows the method of obtaining the backing of
the hip where the plan is not right angled.

Bisect A D in *a*, and from *a* describe the semicircle
A *b* D; draw *a b* parallel to the sides A B, D C, and join
A *b*, D *b*, for the seat of the hip-rafters. From *b* set off on

b A, *b* D the lengths *b d*, *b e*, equal to the height of the roof
b c, and join A *c*, D *d*, for the lengths of the hip-rafters. To
find the backing of the rafter:—In A *c*, take any point *k*,
and draw *k h* perpendicular to A *c*. Through *h* draw *f h g*
perpendicular to A *b*, meeting A B, A D in *f* and *g*. Make
h l equal to *h k*, and join *f l*, *g l*; the *f l g* is the backing
of the hip.

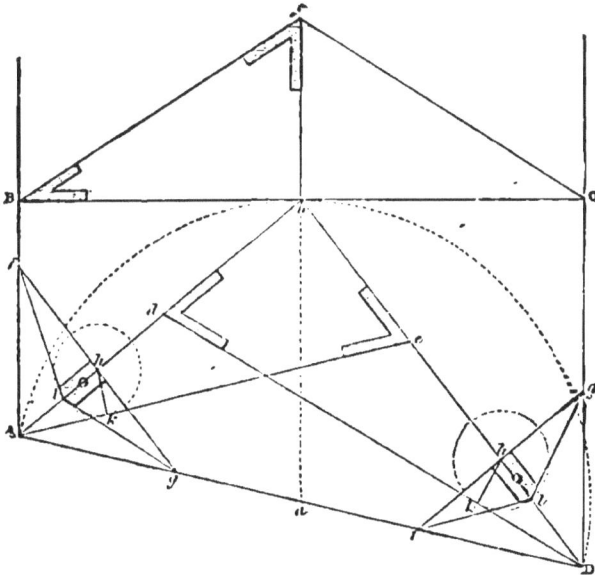

FIG. 61.

Fig. 62 shows how to find the shoulder of purlins:
First, where the purlin has one of its faces in the plane
of the roof, as at E. From *c* as a centre, with any radius,
describe the arc *d g*; and from the opposite extremities of
the diameter, draw *d h*, *g m* perpendicular to B C. From
c and *f*, where the upper adjacent sides of the purlin produced cut the curve, draw *c i. f l* parallel to *d h. g m*; also
draw *c k* parallel to *d h*. From *l* and *i* draw *l m* and *i h*

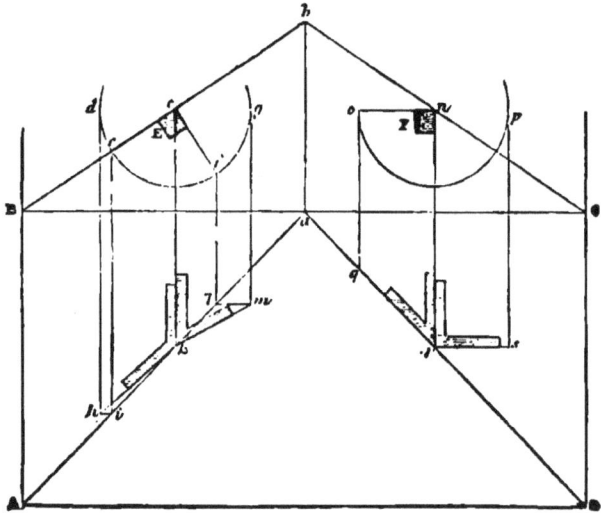

FIG. 62.

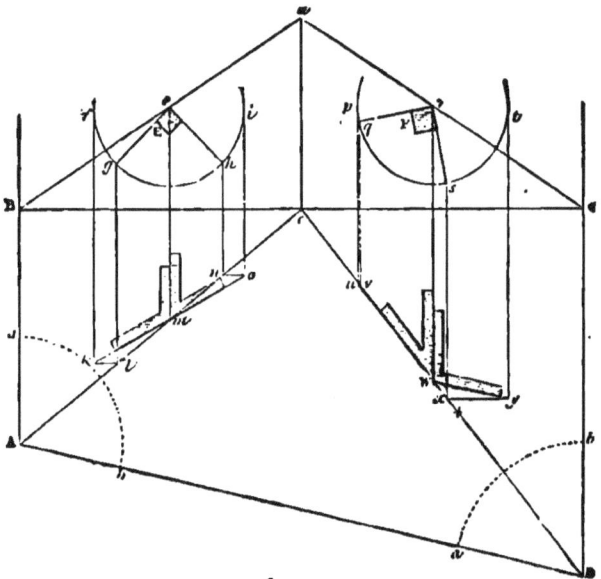

FIG. 63.

parallel to B C, and join *k h, k m*. Then *c k m* is the down
bevel of the purlin, and *c k h* is its side bevel.

When the purlin has two of its sides parallel to the
horizon. This simple case is shown worked out at F. It
requires no explanation.

When the sides of the purlin make various angles with
the horizon. Fig. 63 shows the application of the method
described in Fig. 62 to these cases.

It sometimes happens, particularly in railroad buildings,
that the carpenter is called upon to pierce a circular or
conical roof with a saddle roof, and to accomplish this

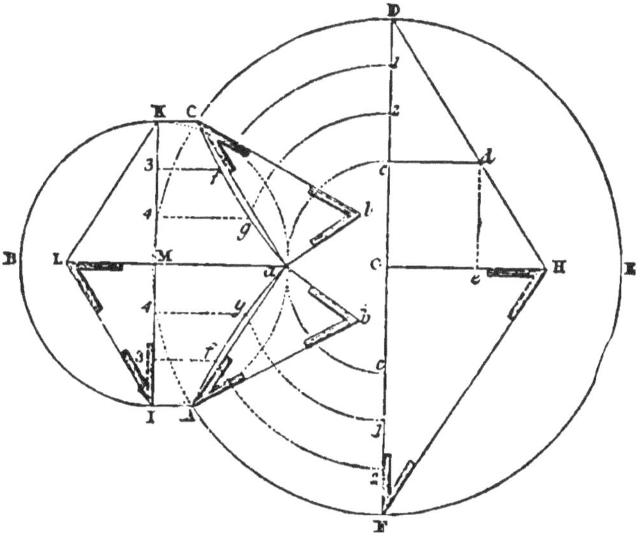

FIG. 64.

economically is often the result of much labor and per-
plexity if a correct method is not at hand.

The following method, shown in Fig. 64, is an excellent

one, and will no doubt be found useful in cases such as mentioned.

Let D H, F H be the common rafters of the conical roof, and K L, I L the common rafters of the smaller roof, both of the same pitch. On G H set up G e equal to M L. the height of the lesser roof, and draw e d parallel to D F, and from d draw c d perpendicular to D F. The triangle D d c, will then by construction be equal to the triangle K L M, and will give the seat and the length and pitch of the common rafter of the smaller roof B. Divide the lines of the seats in both figures, D c, K M, into the same number of equal parts; and through the points of division in E, from G as a centre, describe the curves c a, 2 g, 1 f, and through those in B, draw the lines 3 f, 4 g, M a, parallel to the sides of the roof, and intersecting the curves in f g a. Through these points trace the curves c f g a, A f g a, which give the lines of intersection of the two roofs. Then to find the valley rafters, join c a, A a; and on a erect the lines a b, a b perpendicular to c a and A a, and make them respectively equal to M L; then c b, A b is the length of the valley rafter, very nearly.

Fig. 65 shows how a curved hip-rafter may be obtained. The rafter shown in this instance is ogee in shape, but it makes no difference what shape the common rafter may be, the proper shape and length of hip may be obtained by this method. It will be noticed that one side of the example shown is wider than the other; this is to show that the rule will work correctly where the sides are unequal in width, as well as where they are equal. Let A B c, F E c represent the plan of the roof. F C G the profile of the wide side of the rafter. First, divide this rafter G c into any

number of parts—in this case six. Transfer these points to
the mitre line E B, or, what is the same, the line in the plan
representing the hip rafter. From the points thus estab-
lished in E B, erect perpendiculars indefinitely. With the
dividers take the distance from the points in the line F C,

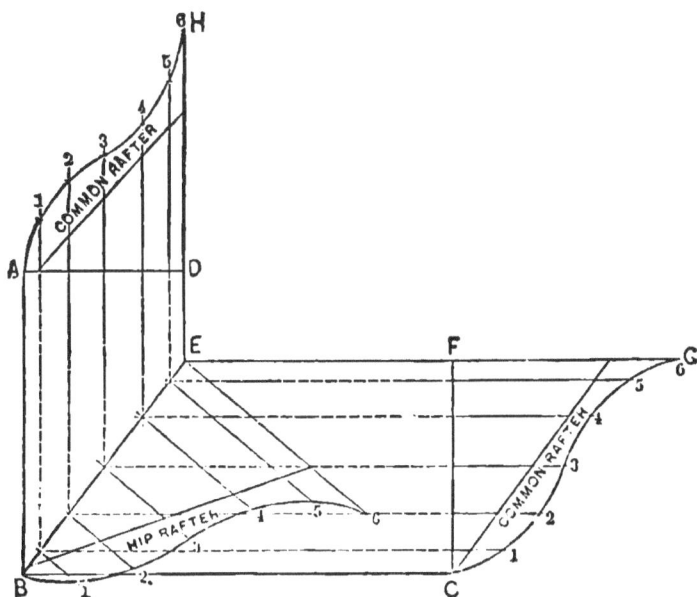

FIG 65

measuring to the points in the profile G C, and set the same
off on corresponding lines, measuring from E B, thus estab-
lishing the points 1, 2, 3, etc.; then a line traced through
these points will be the required hip rafter.

For the common rafter on the narrow side, continue the
lines from E B parallel with the lines of the plan D E and
A B. Draw A D at right angles to these lines. With the
dividers as before, measuring from F C to the points in
G C, set off corresponding distances from A D, thus estab-

lishing the points shown between A and H. A line traced through the points thus obtained will be the line of the rafter on the narrow side. This is supposed to be the return roof of a veranda, but is only shown as an example, for it is not customary to build verandas nowadays with an ogee roof, but with a rafter having a depression or cove in it. For accuracy it would be as well to make nearly twice

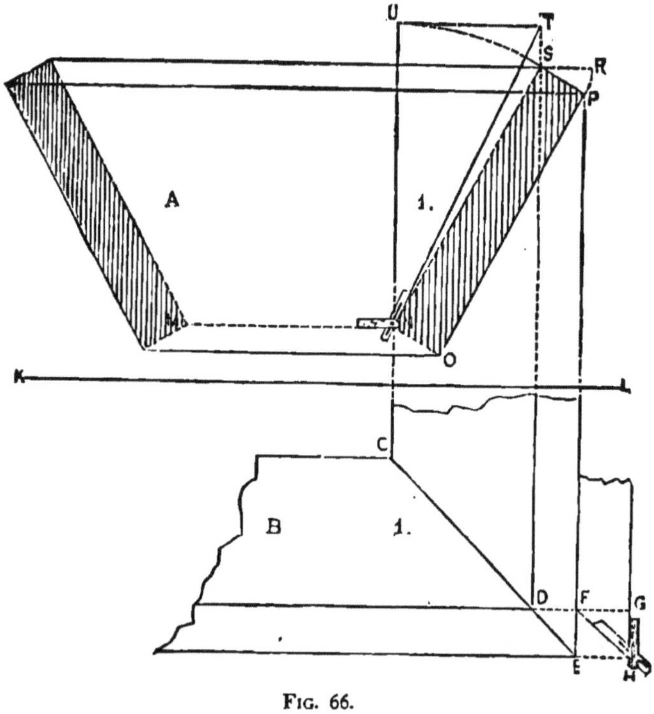

FIG. 66.

the number of divisions shown from 1 to 6, as are there represented.

It has been shown, in the forepart of this work, how the bevels and lines for hoppers may be obtained by the aid of

the square, and it is now proposed to show how the same
results may be obtained by a system of lines. This
method, in many shapes and forms, has been used from
time immemorial by workmen, more particularly by carriage makers to obtain the bevels of splayed seats; the
present way of expressing it, however, is comparatively
recent.

If we make A 1, Fig. 66, represent the elevation of our
hopper, and B 1 a portion of the plan, we proceed as
follows: Lay off N s, which is the bevel of one side, and
N s p o the section of one end.

Place one foot of the dividers at N, and with N s as
radius describe the arc s u, intersecting the right line N u
in the point u. At s erect the perpendicular s т, and draw
the line u т at right angles to N u. Connect N and т;
then the triangle M N т is the end bevel required. The
line N т is the hypothenuse of a right-angled triangle, of
which N u may may be taken for the perpendicular and
u т for the base. To find the mitre of which D E is the
plan, project s and P, as indicated in the plan by the full
lines. With s P as radius and s as centre, describe the arc
P R. In the plan draw D G, on which lay off the distance
s R, measuring from F, as shown by F G. Then ᴳ ʜ F is
the mitre sought.

Fig. 67 shows the rule for finding the bevels for the
sides of the hopper. From M, the point at which E M intersects B C, or the inner face of the hopper, erect the perpendicular M L, intersecting R F, or the upper edge of the
hopper, in the point L. Then ʟ c shows how much longer
the inside edge is required to be than the outside. In the
plan draw т v parallel to s x, making the distance between

the two lines equal to c f of the elevation, or, equal to the thickness of one side.   From the point L in the elevation

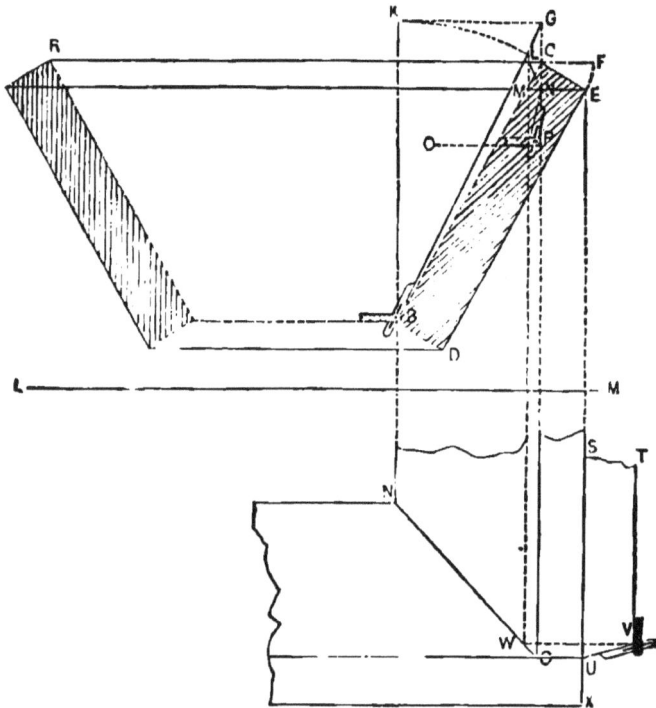

FIG. 67.

drop the line L w, producing it until it cuts the mitre line N o, as shown at w.   From w, at right angles to L w, erect the perpendicular w v, meeting the line T v in the point v.   Connect v and u; then T v u will be the angle sought.   This bevel may be found at once by laying off the thickness of the side from the line E M, as shown by N P in the elevation, and applying the bevel as shown. This course does away with the plan entirely, provided both sides have the same inclination.

There are several other ways by which the same results may be obtained; some of these will no doubt occur to the reader when laying out the lines as shown here.

Fig. 68 exhibits a method of obtaining the correct shape of a veneer for covering the splayed head of a gothic jamb.

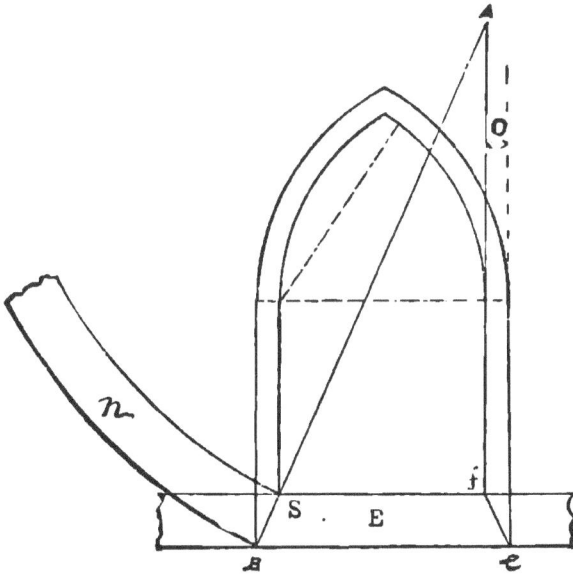

FIG. 68.

E shows the horizontal sill, cf the splay. f A the line of the inside of jamb, o the difference between front and back edges of jamb, B A the line of splay. At the point of junction of the lines B A, fA. set one point of the compasses, and with the radius A B draw the outside curve of n; then with the radius A S draw the inside curve, and n will be the veneer required. This will give the required shape for either side of the head.

PRACTICAL BOOKS FOR PRACTICAL MEN.

The Steel Square and Its Uses. By Hodgson.

Second and Enlarged Edition, - - - - - - - - $1.00

This is the only complete work on The Steel Square and Its Uses ever published. It is thorough, exhaustive, clear and easily understood. Confounding terms and scientific phrases have been religiously avoided where possible, and everything in the book has been made so plain that a boy twelve years of age, possessing ordinary intelligence, can understand it from end to end.

The new edition is illustrated with over seventy-five wood cuts, showing how the Square may be used for solving almost every problem in the whole Art of Carpentry.

Stair-Building Made Easy.

Being a Full and Clear Description of the Art of Building the Bodies, Carriages and Cases for all kinds of Stairs and Steps. Together with Illustrations showing the Manner of Laying Out Stairs, Forming Treads and Risers, Building Cylinders, Preparing Strings, with Instructions for Making Carriages for Common, Platform, Dog-Legged, and Winding Stairs. To which is added an Illustrated Glossary of Terms used in Stair-Building, and Designs for Newels, Balusters, Brackets Stair-Mouldings, and Sections of Hand-Rails. By FRED. T. HODGSON. Cloth, Gilt, - - - - - - $1.00

This work takes hold at the very beginning of the subject, and carries the student along by easy stages, until the entire subject of Stair-Building has been unfolded, so far as ordinary practice can ever require. This book and the one on HAND-RAILING, described below, cover nearly the whole subject of STAIR-BUILDING.

A New System of Hand-Railing.

Or, How to Cut Hand-Railing for Circular and other Stairs, Square from the Plank, without the aid of a Falling Mould. The System is New, Novel, Economic, and Easily Learned. Rules, Instructions, and Working Drawing for Building Rails for Seven Different Kinds of Stairs are given. By AN OLD STAIR-BUILDER. Edited and Corrected by FRED. T. HODGSON. Cloth, Gilt, - - - - - - - - - - - - $1.00

The Workshop Companion.

A Collection of Useful and Reliable Recipes, Rules, Processes, Methods, Wrinkles and Practical Hints for the Household and the Shop. Neatly Bound, - - - - - - - - - - - - - 35c.

This is a book of 164 closely printed pages, forming a Dictionary of Practical Information, for Mechanics, Amateurs, Housekeepers, Farmers, Everybody. It is not a mere collection of newspaper clippings, but a series of original treatises on various subjects, such as Alloys, Cements, Inks, Steel, Signal Lights, Polishing Materials, and the art of Polishing Wood, Metals, etc.; Varnishes, Gilding, Silvering, Bronzing, Lacquering, and the working of Brass, Ivory, Alabaster, Iron, Steel, Glass, etc.

Drawing Instruments.

Being a Treatise on Draughting Instruments, with Rules for their Use and Care, Explanations of Scale, Sectors and Protractors. Together with Memooranda for Draughtsmen, Hints on Purchasing Paper, Ink, Instruments, Pencils, etc. Also a Price List of all materials required by Draughtsmen. Illustrated with Twenty-four Explanatory Illustrations. By FRED. T. HODGSON. Paper, - - - - - - - - - - 25c.

Practical Carpentry.

Illustrated by Over 300 Engravings. Being a Guide to the Correct Working and Laying Out of all kinds of Carpenters' and Joiners' Work. With the solutions of the various problems in Hip-Roofs, Gothic Work, Centering, Splayed Work, Joints and Jointing, Hinging, Dovetailing, Mitering, Timber Splicing, Hopper Work, Skylights, Raking Mouldings, Circular Work, etc., etc., to which is prefixed a thorough treatise on "Carpenter's Geometry." By FRED. T. HODGSON, author of "The Steel Square and Its Uses," "The Builder's Guide and Estimator's Price Book," "The Slide Rule and How to Use It," etc., etc. Cloth, Gilt, - - - - - - - - - $1.00

This is the most complete book of the kind ever published. It is thorough, practical and reliable, and at the same time is written in a style so plain that any workman or apprentice can easily understand it.

Hand Saws.

Their Use, Care and Abuse. How to Select and How to File Them. By FRED. T. HODGSON, author of "The Steel Square and Its Uses," "The Builder's Guide and Estimator's Price Book," "Practical Carpentry," etc., etc. Illustrated by Over 75 Engravings. Being a Complete Guide for Selecting. Using and Filing all kinds of Hand Saws, Back Saws, Compass and Key-hole Saws, Web, Hack and Butcher's Saws; showing the Shapes, Forms, Angles, Pitches and Sizes of Saw Teeth suitable for all kinds of Saws, and for all kinds of Wood, Bone, Ivory and Metal; together with Hints and Suggestions on the choice of Files, Saw Sets, Filing Clamps, and other matters pertaining to the care and management of all classes of hand and other small saws. Cloth, Gilt, - - - - - - - - - $1.00

The work is intended more particularly for operative Carpenters, Joiners, Cabinet Makers, Carriage Builders and Wood Workers generally, amateurs or professionals.

Plaster : How to Make, and How to Use.

Illustrated with numerous engravings in the text, and Three Plates, giving some Forty Figures of Ceilings, Centrepieces, Cornices, Panels, and Soffits. Being a complete guide for the plasterer, in the preparation and application of all kinds of Plaster, Stucco, Portland Cements, Hydraulic Cements, Lime of Tiel, Rosendale and other Cements. To which is added an Illustrated Glossary of Technical Terms used by plasterers, with hints and suggestions regarding the working, mixing and preparation of scagliola and colored mortars of various kinds. Cloth, Gilt, - - - - - - $1.00

Just the book for Plasterers, Bricklayers, Masons, Builders, Architects and Engineers.

The Builder's Guide and Estimator's Price Book.

Being a Compilation of Current Prices of Lumber, Hardware, Glass, Plumbers' Supplies, Paints, Slates, Stones, Limes, Cements, Bricks, Tin, and other Building Materials; also, Prices of Labor, and Cost of Performing the Several Kinds of Work Required in Building. Together with Prices of Doors, Frames, Sashes, Stairs, Mouldings, Newels, and other Machine Work. To which is appended a large number of Building Rules, Data, Tables, and Useful Memoranda, with a Glossary of Architectural and Building Terms. By FRED. T. HODGSON, Editor of "The Builder and Wood-Worker," Author of "The Steel Square and Its Uses," etc., etc. 12mo., Cloth, - $2.00

Hints for Cabinet Makers, Upholsterers, and Furniture Men.

Hints and Practical Information for Cabinet-Makers, Upholsterers, and Furniture Men generally. Together with a description of all kinds of Finishing, with full directions therefor, Varnishes, Polishes, Stains for Wood, Dyes for Wood, Gilding and Silvering, Receipts for the Factory, Lacquers, Metals, Marbles, etc.; Pictures, Engravings, etc.; Miscellaneous. This work contains an immense amount of the most useful information for those who are engaged in Manufacture, Superintendence, or Construction of Furniture or Wood Work of any kind. It is one of the Cheapest and Best Books ever published, and contains over 1,000 Hints, Suggestions, Methods, and Descriptions of Tools, Appliances and Materials. All the Recipes, Rules, and Directions have been carefully Revised and Corrected by Practical Men of great experience, so that they will be found thoroughly trustworthy. Cloth, Gilt, - - - - - - - - - - - - - - - - $1.00

Mechanical Draughting.

The Student's Illustrated Guide to Practical Draughting. A series of Practical Instructions for Machinists, Mechanics, Apprentices, and Students at Engineering Establishments and Technical Institutes. By T. P. PEMBERTON, Draughtsman and Mechanical Engineer. Illustrated with numerous engravings. Cloth, Gilt. - - - - - - - - - - - $1.00

This is a simple but thorough book, by a draughtsman of twenty-five years' experience. It is intended for beginners and self-taught students, as well as for those who pursue the study under the direction of a teacher.

Lectures in a Workshop.

By T. P. PEMBERTON, formerly Associate Editor of the "Technologist;" Author of "The Student's Illustrated Guide to Practical Draughting." With an appendix containing the famous papers by Whitworth "On Plane Metallic Surfaces or True Planes;" "On an Uniform System of Screw Threads;" "Address to the Institution of Mechanical Engineers, Glasgow;" "On Standard Decimal Measures of Length." Cloth, Gilt, - - - $1.00

We have here a sprightly, fascinating book, full of valuable hints, interesting anecdotes and sharp sayings. It is not a compilation of dull sermons or dry mathematics, but a live, readable book. The papers by Whitworth, now first made accessible to the American reader, form the basis of our modern systems of accurate work.

How to Use The Microscope.

By JOHN PHIN. Fifth Edition. Greatly enlarged, with over eighty Illustrations in the Text, and six full page Engravings, printed on heavy tint paper. Cloth, Gilt, - - - - - - - - - - - - $1.00

This is not a book describing *what may be seen* by the microscope, but a simple and practical work, telling how to use the instrument in its application to the arts. It has been prepared for the use of those who, having no knowledge of the use of the microscope, or, indeed, of any scientific apparatus, desire simple and practical instruction in the best methods of managing the instrument and preparing objects.

A New Book for Bee-Keepers.

A Dictionary of Practical Apiculture, giving the correct meaning of nearly Five Hundred Terms, according to the usage of the best writers. Intended as a Guide to Uniformity of Expression amongst Bee-Keepers. With Numerous Illustrations, Notes, and Practical Hints. By JOHN PHIN, Author of "How to Use the Microscope," etc. Editor of the "Young Scientist." Price, Cloth, Gilt, . - - - - - - - - - - 50 cts.

This work gives not only the correct meaning of five hundred different words, specially used in bee-keeping, but an immense amount of valuable information under the different headings. The labor expended upon it has been very great, the definitions having been gathered from the mode in which the words are used by our best writers on bee-keeping, and from the Imperial, Richardson's, Skeat's, Websters, Worcester's and other English Dictionaries. The technical information relating to matters connected with bee-keeping has been gathered from the Technical Dictionaries of Brande, Muspratt, Ure, Wagner, Watts, and others. Under the heads *Bee. Comb, Glucose, Honey, Race, Species. Sugar*, *Wax* and others, it brings together a large number of important facts and figures which are now scattered through our bee-literature, and through costly scientific works, and are not easily found when wanted. Here they can be referred to at once under the proper head.

How to Become a Good Mechanic.

Intended as a Practical Guide to Self-taught Men ; telling What to Study ; What Books to Use ; How to Begin ; What Difficulties will be Met ; How to Overcome Them. In a word, how to carry on such a Course of Self-instruction as will enable the Young Mechanic to rise from the bench to something higher. Paper, - - - - - - - - - - - 15 cts.

This is not a book of "goody-goody" advice, neither is it an advertisement of any special system, nor does it advocate any hobby. It gives plain, practical advice in regard to acquiring that knowledge which alone can enable a young man engaged in any profession or occupation connected with the industrial arts to attain a position higher than that of a mere workman.

Cements and Glue.

A Practical Treatise on the Preparation and Use of all Kinds of Cements, Glue, and Paste. By JOHN PHIN, Editor of the "Young Scientist" and the "American Journal of Microscopy." Stiff Covers, - - - 25 cts.

Hints for Painters, Decorators and Paperhangers.

Being a selection of Useful Rules, Data, Memoranda, Methods and Suggestions for House, Ship. and Furniture Painting, Paperhanging, Gilding, Color Mixing, and other matters Useful and Instructive to Painters and Decorators. Prepared with Special Reference to the Wants of Amateurs. By an OLD HAND. - - - - - - - - - - - 25 cts.

Any of these books will be sent post paid to any address on receipt of price.

Shooting on the Wing.

Plain Directions for Acquiring the Art of Shooting on the Wing. With Useful Hints concerning all that relates to Guns and Shooting, and particularly in regard to the art of Loading so as to Kill. To which has been added several Valuable and hitherto Secret Recipes, of Great Practical Importance to the Sportsman. By an Old Gamekeeper.

12mo., Cloth, Gilt Title. -   -   -   75 cents.

The Pistol as a Weapon of Defence,

In the House and on the Road.

12mo., Cloth. -   -   -   -   50 cents.

This work aims to instruct the peaceable and law-abiding citizens in the best means of protecting themselves from the attacks of the brutal and the lawless, and is the only practical book published on this subject. Its contents are as follows: The Pistol as a Weapon of Defence.—The Carrying of Fire-Arms.—Different kinds of Pistols in Market; How to Choose a Pistol.—Ammunition, different kinds; Powder, Caps, Bullets, Copper Cartridges, etc.—Best form of Bullet.— How to Load.—Best Charge for Pistols.—How to regulate the Charge.—Care of the Pistol; how to Clean it.—How to Handle and Carry the Pistol.—How to Learn to Shoot.—Practical use of the Pistol; how to Protect yourself and how to Disable your antagonist.

Lightning Rods.

Plain Directions for the Construction and Erection of Lightning Rods. By John Phin, C. E., editor of "The Young Scientist," author of "Chemical History of the Six Days of the Creation," etc. Second Edition. Enlarged and Fully Illustrated.

12mo., Cloth, Gilt Title. -   -   -   50 cents.

This is a simple and practical little work, intended to convey just such information as will enable every property owner to decide whether or not his buildings are thoroughly protected. It is not written in the interest of any patent or particular article of manufacture, and by following its directions, any ordinarily skilful mechanic can put up a rod that will afford perfect protection, and that will not infringe any patent. Every owner of a house or barn ought to procure a copy.

THE WORKSHOP COMPANION.

A Collection of Useful and Reliable Recipes, Rules, Processes, Methods, Wrinkles, and Practical Hints,

FOR THE HOUSEHOLD AND THE SHOP.

CONTENTS.

164 closely-printed pages, neatly bound.   Sent by mail for 36 cents (postage stamps received).